Activating Creativity

Insights and Wisdom of

MacArthur Fellows

It seems to be one of the paradoxes of creativity that
in order to think originally, we must familiarize
ourselves with the ideas of others.

George Kneller

Leslie A. Hennessy Ph.D.

Sherwood Publications, Colorado Springs (catalyst.rk@icloud.com)

Ordering information:
All royalties from book sales are donated to Canine Companions for Independence (CCI), a 501(c)(3) nonprofit that provides highly trained service dogs free of charge to individuals with disabilities. Donations to CCI are maximized when books are purchased through lulu.com. Books are also available from Amazon.com, BarnesandNoble.com, and Ingramcontent.com

Educational & Quantity Sales: contact Sherwood Publications

ISBN: 978-1-365-65002-4

Printed in the United States of America

CONTENTS

CHAPTER ONE

INTRODUCTION

Why should anyone be interested in creativity? The answer is simple. Creativity is the physical manifestation of human ingenuity and pursuing it is pleasurable, exciting, and fun. Additionally, participating in creative projects can make human creators feel more alive and productive. Mihaly Csikszentmihalyi, an eminent researcher in creativity, says, "Of all human activities, creativity comes closest to providing the fulfillment we all hope to get in our lives. Call it full-blast living."[1]

Beyond adding joy to life, creativity is also an important aspect of effective living because it supports humankind's success on the planet and promotes the advancement of civilization. A changing world requires creative responses to solve complex problems, so individuals need to learn how to engage their creative abilities to deal with a range of domestic and global issues.

What sorts of pursuits are creative? Creativity can describe momentous accomplishments in established fields such as art, science, economics, or commerce. This is the sort of

---

[1] M. Csikszentmihalyi, "The Creative Personality," *Psychology Today* (July/August, 1996): 36.

creativity that many individuals consider when they think about the subject. However, there is another form of creativity that is manifested when individuals devise novel ways to modestly improve daily functioning by refining how they approach challenges in life. Both types of creativity are important.

The Purpose of This Book

History has recorded evidence that humans have long been creative and that ancient civilizations had the ability to solve problems imaginatively. However, the sages of ancient times believed that the gods bestowed creative ability only on chosen individuals. Since creativity was shrouded in mystery and was deemed a *gift* from the muses,[2] individuals in past eras, and even some individuals in present times, consider creativity to be a capacity that is available to only a few. In reality, all individuals have the ability to be creative, and anyone who is willing to learn how to activate, develop, and sustain creative processes and habits can develop their skills.

The purpose of this book is to help readers better understand how creative outcomes can be achieved. In order to accomplish this goal, the book defines the strategies and processes that can enhance individual creative ability and describes the characteristics and habits that may increase creative potential. In addition, the book provides concrete suggestions that demonstrate how the development of creative thinking skills

---

[2] T. I. Lubart, "Creativity" in *Thinking and Problem Solving*, 2nd ed., ed. R. J. Sternberg (San Diego CA: Academic Press, 1994), 289-332.

can lead to creative outcomes. However, while this book can serve as a roadmap to improve creativity, the strategies and processes of creativity are intensely personal. As a result, readers should always be open to discovering additional ways to expand their own creative processes.

The Underlying Research That Supports This Book

Data-driven analysis is important when discussing creativity because theorizing without data is imaginative but not necessarily credible. Arthur Conan Doyle (physician and writer; 1859-1930) says it well: "It is a capital mistake to theorize before one has data. Insensibly one begins to twist facts to suit theories, instead of theories to suit facts."[3]

In keeping with Doyle's assertion, the information in this book is grounded in data and not conjecture. The basis of the evidence presented is dissertation research that I completed in 2014. The study investigated the manner in which creative thinkers activate, develop, and sustain their creativity through their decision making. [4]

Dissertation Methodology

At the heart of the dissertation research are the personal insights and recollections of a group of individuals recognized for their creativity. These individuals are all recipients of the

---

[3] A. C. Doyle, *Classic adventures of Sherlock Holmes*, (New York, NY: Barnes & Noble Books, 2001), 157.
[4] L. A. Hennessy, Decision Making and Creativity: A Qualitative Study of MacArthur Fellows (dissertation, University of San Diego, 2014).

MacArthur Foundation's award for creativity. They are known as MacArthur Fellows.

MacArthur Foundation

The John D. and Catherine T. MacArthur Foundation is the 12th-largest private foundation in the United States. Based in Chicago, the foundation makes grants to support nonprofit organizations in Chicago, across the United States, and in approximately 50 countries. The foundation has assets totaling more than $6 billion and provides approximately $250 million annually in awards. The foundation's stated aim is to support creative people, effective institutions, and influential networks building a more just, verdant, and peaceful world.

One of the programs that the MacArthur Foundation supports is the MacArthur Fellows Program, which makes annual awards to about two dozen creative individuals in diverse fields. Each award is for $625,000 paid over a 5-year time frame. The awards are commonly referred to as *genius grants* and represent the foundation's reward for an individual's originality, insight, and potential in a specific field. The award comes without restrictions or obligations. The foundation does not require future work on any particular project or in any specific field. Additionally, the foundation does not require any reporting on how the award money is spent. According to the foundation, the award is presented in the belief that creative people, left to their own devices and unhindered by reporting requirements and other bureaucratic oversight, will have the opportunity to focus on their work and will develop additional creative insights and outcomes. Since 1981, approximately 1,000 individuals have been named MacArthur Fellows.

Dissertation Sample and Data Collection

All MacArthur Foundation award winners have made significant contributions to their respective fields by creating artistic representations in literature, music, theater, art or other fields; however, the research participants chosen for this dissertation study were limited to award winners who have founded and led either a nonprofit or for-profit organization. Moreover, the selected award winners use their creativity to address societal problems. They are skilled at linking human endeavors, bridging unlikely fields, and creatively expanding the boundaries of human knowledge.

Data collection for the dissertation involved face-to-face interviews with eight MacArthur Fellows.[5] Brief biographies follow.

Dr. Saul Griffith

> MacArthur Foundation Fellow: Class of 2007. Dr. Saul Griffith is a prolific inventor interested in developing useful products, including robotic orthotics, robots controlled by air, computational manufacturing and design tools, conformable tanks for more environmentally-friendly vehicles, solar tracking components, and thermally adaptive materials. His company, Otherlab, also develops hands-on education for teaching science and engineering.

---

[5] Seven of the interviewees share their insights in this book.

Dr. Wes Jackson

MacArthur Foundation Fellow: Class of 1992. In 1976, Dr. Wes Jackson founded The Land Institute in Salina, Kansas. The Land Institute is known for its pioneering work in Natural Systems Agriculture. Directed by a team of agronomists and ecologists, the organization focuses on developing perennial grains, pulses (part of the legume family), and oilseed bearing plants that are grown in ecologically intensified, diverse crop mixtures known as perennial polycultures. The goal is to create an agriculture system that mimics natural systems in order to produce food and reduce or eliminate the negative impacts of industrial agriculture.

Mr. James Fruchterman

MacArthur Foundation Fellow: Class of 2006. Jim Fruchterman is the founder and CEO of Benetech, a socially oriented technology organization that puts existing technologies to use in innovative ways. Benetech has created a web-based library of scanned books to provide people with visual or learning disabilities downloadable access to a dramatically increased volume of printed materials. Martus, another initiative, provides a secure computer-based reporting system to assist the human rights sector in collecting, safeguarding, and disseminating information about human rights violations.

Ms. Susan Sygall

MacArthur Foundation Fellow: Class of 2000. Susan Sygall co-founded and leads Mobility International USA (MIUSA), a nonprofit organization headquartered in Eugene, Oregon. The organization provides expertise, skills training, and advocacy to advance the rights of people with disabilities. The goal of the organization is to encourage individuals with disabilities to fully participate in society. MIUSA also supports global leadership at its annual Women's Institute on Leadership and Disability (WILD) conference.

Dr. Victoria Hale

MacArthur Foundation Fellow: Class of 2006. Dr. Victoria Hale is the founder of Medicines 360 and currently serves on its board of directors. The organization's mission is to expand access to medical services for women around the world. Part nonprofit and part for-profit, the organization develops and distributes medicines and medical devices. The result is that low-income women around the world have the opportunity to access more healthcare choices.

Ms. Wilma Subra

MacArthur Foundation Fellow: Class of 1999. Committed to protecting the environment and the health and safety of citizens, Wilma Subra founded the Subra Company in New Iberia, Louisiana, in 1981. The chemistry lab and environmental consulting firm provides technical research and evaluation to ordinary citizens to help them understand, cope with, and combat environmental issues in their communities. These services, which are often provided pro bono, support community efforts to fight environmental polluters.

Mr. Aaron Dworkin

MacArthur Foundation Fellow: Class of 2005. Aaron Dworkin is a passionate advocate for excellence in arts education and inclusion in the performing arts. He is the founder of the Detroit-based Sphinx Organization, which is dedicated to supporting minority participation and careers in classical music. This nonprofit has changed the lives of many African American and Latino musicians and has altered the landscape of classical music in America.

In the interviews, the participants share their insights and ideas about their own creative practices. Specifically, participants report on the strategies and processes that encourage and promote their creative thinking and problem solving. Additionally, participants discuss their personal characteristics and habits that they believe reinforce their creative success.

In this book, all quotes by the interviewees are taken from the dissertation. To augment data from the interviews, additional stories about creative thinking that come from history are also included to further identify and reinforce the way novel outcomes develop in society.

Educational Benefits of This Book

Individuals who are curious about creativity and would like guidance on how to enhance their creative abilities may find this book educational. More specifically, those who are involved in science, business, social reform, and teaching can benefit because as they gain a better understanding of creativity, they will learn how to activate, develop, and sustain their abilities. Additionally, team participants or leaders can improve their capacity for creativity.

An essential point to remember is that individuals of any age can benefit from understanding the wisdom of the creative MacArthur Fellows. Their advice on creativity is easy to comprehend and most anyone can adopt their strategies and processes to enhance outcomes.

CHAPTER TWO

UNDERSTANDING CREATIVITY

Evidence of creativity permeates history. Even before the invention of writing, artisans created paintings, statuary, and jewelry for the rich and as a tribute to the gods they worshipped. As early as 1250 BCE, during the Trojan War, field commanders were extolled for their creative strategies that resulted in battle victory. About 650 BCE, lyric poets and ancient playwrights were celebrated for their creative work, and philosophers, scientists, inventors, and doctors were praised for their innovative ideas and processes that produced new products, knowledge, and skills.

In present times, creativity extends to strategies in business, novel outcomes in dealing with social issues, and all manner of innovation in products and services. Generally, creativity involves generating improvements in individual quality of life or societal function. In addition, measurements of organizational success are often equated with creativity.

Creativity can also be an important tool in solving problems. It is potentially the only way to make significant gains on problems that are seemingly intractable and continue to perplex humans. In effect, the world's most confounding problems would have already been solved if the application of conformist and standardized solutions could get results. Perhaps J. P. Guilford says it best: "The preservation of our way of life and our future security depend upon our most important natural resources: our intellectual abilities and, more particularly, our creative abilities."[6]

What Is Creativity?

Creativity, as described in this book, is a combination of imagination, ingenuity, and inventiveness that results in innovative outcomes that are artful and clever and favor originality, appropriateness, and utility. While a notion of newness surrounds the concept of creativity, there must also be a societal judgment that the newness is of value to the culture. In fact, creativity and value are closely aligned. Novel outcomes without cultural validation of worth are seldom celebrated. It should be noted that the connection to newness is a decidedly Western societal approach to creativity. Other societies often prioritize utility over originality.

This book also acknowledges Todd Lubart's practical definition of creativity. He notes that creativity is the ability to produce novel, appropriate work in either a tangible or intangible form.[7] Furthermore, Lubart suggests that while there is no absolute standard for assessing creativity, creative solutions are likely to produce *stand-apart* work that has not formerly been

---

[6] J. P. Guilford, *Intelligence, Creativity, and their Educational Implications* (San Diego, CA: Knapp, 1969), 15.

[7] T. I. Lubart, "Creativity" in *Thinking and Problem Solving*, 2nd ed., ed. R. J. Sternberg (San Diego CA: Academic Press, 1994), 289-332.

---

produced and is likely to provoke surprise in the viewer because the work is more than the next logical step. In other words, creative work should be original, reveal quality, demonstrate utility, and expand understanding.

Lubart's definition suggests an important point. While creativity may be hard to define, creative work is consistently recognizable. Interestingly, individuals are able to spot creativity in various forms; however, settling on a universal definition is more difficult.

Using Lubart's definition of creativity, individuals are only considered to be creative as a result of the work produced. For instance, Mozart would have not been considered creative without the physical evidence of creativity—his symphonies. However, it is important to note that while the outcomes are the definitive measures of creativity, it is the mental process that is the genesis of the creative activity.

Lubart further suggests that creative individuals are likely to demonstrate their innovative abilities on a regular basis. Said another way, creativity is not a chance occurrence. Rather, it is a propensity to see the world in a way that predicts multiple occasions where creative ideas and solutions will be proposed and implemented.

Big C or Little c Creativity

Big C creativity is defined as memorable, defining, and far-reaching outcomes that change the course of fields, disciplines, and industries. Many of the stories and examples in this book deal with such outcomes. They are important because such creativity can affect many people—communities, cultures, and other global groups. An example of big C creativity is the invention of the steam engine, which revolutionized various forms of travel, energy production, and manufacturing; providing the basis for numerous industries.

Another sort of creativity, known as little c creativity, is also part of the human experience. This brand of creativity represents everyday life enhancements that can enrich human existence and improve lives. It may not lead to the creation of new products or mega deals between international groups, but it represents a heightened personal experience of creativity.

To better understand little c creativity, consider the following example. Canine Companions for Independence,[8] a national nonprofit organization, was looking for ways to solicit donations to help refurbish its residential dorm rooms at its regional training center in the Southwest region of the United States. A volunteer considered the idea of a gift registry (bridal/baby) where specific products are earmarked as desirable and friends can purchase products in various quantities and for a range of prices. Borrowing from the concept of registries, the organization adapted a registry at a local store to meet its need for donated goods. The idea was a success; products specified on the store registry were purchased and donated.

---

[8] Canine Companions for Independence is a nonprofit organization that enhances the lives of people with disabilities by providing highly trained assistance dogs free of charge to individuals with disabilities.

While it is tempting to suggest that there is more value to humankind in the activation of big C creativity, this outlook is limiting. Also, the comparison is moot. The ways to promote big C creativity and little c creativity are the same. Therefore, while this book generally describes big C creativity, little c creativity can also be jumpstarted using the same strategies and processes.

Creativity—Available to Everyone

Creativity is present in all individuals[9] and can be nurtured through understanding and practice.[10] Therefore, if creativity is to be an engine for the improvement of civilization and culture, individuals of all ages should be encouraged to activate, develop, and sustain creativity in their personal and professional lives.

Since many people are convinced that only a limited number of gifted individuals have the capacity to be creative, the first step to better understanding creativity is to question this assertion and provide society with evidence that creativity can be nurtured. Imagine what could be accomplished if creativity was promoted to center stage in everyday life and individuals were given a mandate to pursue original thinking in all realms. Imagine the improvements if individuals were determined to solve problems creatively rather than gloss over problems and

---

[9] N. K. Mildrum, "Creativity Reigns," *Education Digest* 66, no. 2 (2000): 33-38.
[10] S. L. Hunsaker, "Outcomes of Creativity Training Programs," *Gifted Child Quarterly* 49, no. 4 (2005): 292-99.

pass them off to others—other people, other countries, other generations.

It is also important to note that creativity is not age bound. Despite studies that have suggested that most significant creative achievements are produced early in a career, a new and comprehensive study has shown that creativity is not related to age.[11]

Problem Solving—Maximize, Satisfice, or Compromise

There are three common ways to reach a problem solution—maximize, satisfice, or compromise. Understanding the definition of each methodology helps individuals better assess a resolution's worth.

Maximize

Maximization is a type of decision making that is characterized by a search for the *best* option. Best refers to the most advantageous set of circumstances for all concerned in any situation. Maximizing assumes that a thorough search of options will yield one best choice. This term is often associated with capitalism and used in the context of maximizing profit, but may also refer to any situation that may be optimized.

---

[11] B. Carey, "When it Comes to Success, Age is Really Just a Number," *New York Times,* November 3, 2016.

Satisfice

Nobel Prize winner Herbert Simon coined the term satisficing.[12] It represents a combination of two words: satisfy and suffice. Satisficing, as a strategy for human problem solving, is the decision that is made when the person or entity responsible for the decision has identified a decision alternative that meets or surpasses an acceptable decision threshold. In satisficing situations, decision makers evaluate options until one that is *good enough* is uncovered. In reality, satisficing is often operative when a decision is constrained by time or money.

The development of the automobile engine is an example of satisficing. As internal combustion engines became popular for use in automobiles, engineers recognized that more efficient engines could be designed by increasing engine compression ratios. However, when compression ratios were increased, violent engine knocking occurred. The engine design was not at fault; rather, the problem resulted from inadequacy in the fuel. Design engineers lived with this problem—creating a satisficing engine design—until improvements in fuel refining and the addition of tetraethyl lead provided antiknock qualities. Only then could engines be designed more efficiently with higher compression ratios.

Compromise

In the decision making arena, compromising is a strategy agreed upon by all parties where outcomes are not maximized.

---

[12] H. A. Simon, "Rational Choice and the Structure of the Environment," *Psychological Review* 63, no. 2 (1956): 136.

In a true compromise, parties give up aspects of their desired outcomes equally so there is simply a tradeoff of outcomes. Although compromise can result in agreement, no outcomes are maximized and the plan is suboptimal.

The following case illustrates the shortcomings of compromise. In an estate settlement, two adult children tried to equitably divide their mother's personal property. Both heirs wanted a certain pair of earrings. Not being able to agree on who should take the earrings, they accepted that they needed to compromise. Their compromise was that each heir should take one of the earrings. This compromise, while possibly accepted as fair, did not really solve the dilemma in a way that made anyone happy.

Creativity Favors Maximizing

Creative solutions favor maximizing strategies. While it is often difficult to know when a strategy has been maximized, careful analysis of a problem and having the patience to search for creative solutions can enhance chances of choosing optimal solutions. Additionally, not settling for incremental improvement can support maximizing efforts.

The work of Jim Fruchterman (MacArthur Fellow: Class of 2006) provides an example of how opportunities may be maximized. Jim founded and leads the nonprofit organization Benetech. Benetech is a technology company focused on promoting social change by putting existing technologies to use in innovative ways. Jim strives to help nonprofit organizations accomplish their goals by adapting technology for specific uses in the sector.

Benetech pursues projects that for-profit organizations are ignoring or have discarded. In some cases, for-profits have developed the technology 99% of the way, but they are not willing to take the product to market because the technology in question would not make money or would not make enough money to be viable in terms of corporate profit goals. However, Jim and his staff are willing to take over the development of the technology and go, according to Jim, the last *social* mile to bring a product to market and provide a positive social impact.

According to Jim, in his search for creative products, he needs to consciously look for creative ways of doing things—not just settling for incremental process improvements. Jim points out that any problem is likely to have multiple solutions and that accepting a solution that simply works will not generally maximize creativity.

Jim's creative concept of a library is an example of his ability to doggedly pursue creative results. As Jim considered how libraries could better support individuals with disabilities, he concluded that the concept of a traditional library that involves hardcopy books would not serve the needs of many in the disability community because individuals with visual impairments, physical disabilities, or learning disabilities cannot always read traditional books. A better solution would be to develop a library online that would provide audio content.

Next, Jim considered how the content (i.e., books) could be made available to clients in audio form. This goal could have been accomplished by having library staff accept the job of uploading audio for clients. However, while this was one solution, Jim did not settle for the conventional approach; rather, he demonstrated his tenacity to discover an even more creative solution—a maximizing solution.

As Jim considered the library design, he contemplated the model provided by Napster, an Internet company that introduced peer-to-peer sharing of audio files. Based on his interest in the Napster model, Jim conceived of a new type of library that would accept input (audio files) from its clients. Jim's new type of library, called Bookshare, allows library patrons to upload their own material, permitting the library to grow more quickly and more economically. Additionally, his approach gives clients a bigger say in what content is uploaded.

The Origin of Creative Ideas

Creativity may emerge in two distinct ways. New products and processes may be developed to meet needs that society has acknowledged. When such needs are expressed, creative individuals must give definition to the project, refine the parameters, and develop the outcome. In other situations, needs have not been understood and noted by society, and individuals are unaware that a product or process could be helpful to them. In such situations, the needs must be acknowledged and defined, and so creative problem solving has an extra phase: It must begin by imagining and articulating the need that society can effectively utilize.

Creativity in Response to a Need

When society acknowledges a problem that needs to be solved, the challenge is generally loosely defined, yet it requires creative individuals to develop and implement a solution. The development of bar codes is a revealing example of creativity triggered in response to a known problem. In his book, *Eureka*, Weightman tells the story of Joe Woodland, a graduate of Drexel Institute of Technology.[13] Woodland understood that inventory accuracy was a pressing issue for various businesses, especially the grocery industry. He set out to solve the problem by creating a numerical coding system to easily distinguish products.

Woodland considered the simplicity of Morse code and how its dots and dashes could convey messages. How, he wondered, could discrete products be inscribed with data that could identify them? How could such information be read and recorded like Morse code?

Woodland's epiphany came when he was sitting on a beach. While idly drawing his fingers through the sand, he observed the patterns that were created by his fingers. From this experience, Woodland recognized that he could develop a code using lines of different widths. This revelation led to the development of the bar code industry.

---

[13] G. Weightman, *Eureka: How Invention Happens* (New Haven, CT: Yale University Press, 2015).

Woodland received the patent for the bar code in 1952. However, at that time, he was only able to demonstrate his technological advancement using a powerful incandescent bulb and an oscilloscope to read the bar code symbols. However, once a bar code scanner was commercially available, bar codes were added to identify many types of products. Basically, the same technology is used to scan groceries, railroad cars, library books, in-transit luggage, and manufacturing parts and subassemblies.

While Weightman's history of the invention of the bar code acknowledges the creativity of Joe Woodland, the story also illustrates an important lesson: Creativity may initially appear to involve the vision and action of a single individual, but, after deeper analysis, it may become clear that the final creative product is actually the result of an integration of work accomplished by additional creative individuals. For example, Woodland's bar code would not be commercially viable until George J. Laurer created the Uniform Product Code (UPC) in 1973 and a reliable bar code reader was made available to the industry in the following year. Sir Karl Popper (an Austrian-British philosopher and professor of science; 1902-1994) reinforces the idea that multiple creative individuals are generally involved in producing an innovative product. According to him, "The notion that one can begin anything at all from scratch, free from the past, or unindebted to others, could not conceivably be more wrong." [14]

---

[14] B. Magee, *Popper* (London: Woburn Press, 1974), 69.

Present-day needs also generate appeals to solve problems. The need to prevent or cure diseases continues to prompt searches for vaccines and other medicines. Shortages and the environmental shortcomings of fossil fuels encourage research into a variety of fuel alternatives that can be used to power homes, automobiles, and commerce. Since societal problems continue to emerge, the need for creative solutions will persist.

Creation to Fulfill an Unnamed Need

There are many documented cases where society was not aware that it might conceivably need a new product or outcome. For example, the populace did not know that it needed electricity or an airplane until creative individuals proposed such advancements. The microwave oven is an example of a technology that society didn't realize it needed. The history of this invention exemplifies how and why such creative technologies evolve and are introduced into the market.

During WWII, the development of radar was important to the war effort. Radar was an object-detection system that used electromagnetic waves in the radio or microwaves domain that reflected off an object, providing location and speed of the target. The magnetron tube used microwaves to produce the high-power output required in the radar equipment. Microwaves are found in the non-ionizing portion of the energy spectrum, which means that they do not detach charged particles and produce atoms with an unbalanced plus or minus charge. As a result, microwaves produce heat but not radioactivity.

After the war, companies that had developed technologies used by the military were looking for ways to turn their wartime technologies into peacetime profits. Percy Spencer, a Raytheon Company research scientist, was testing a new vacuum tube when he noticed that a candy bar in his pocket had melted. Perplexed by the occurrence, and believing that the microwaves from his experiments were involved, he set out some corn kernels near the functioning magnetron tubes. As he watched, the corn kernels cracked and exploded—producing popcorn—a soon-to-be microwave favorite.

Cooking with microwaves gained widespread acceptance beginning in 1967 when Amana, a division of Raytheon, introduced the Radarange microwave oven for kitchen countertop use. The Radarange became a widely accepted substitute for traditional stovetop cooking, and the rest—as is often said—is history. Now, most kitchens have a microwave oven, and cooking using microwaves is customary.

The Role of Luck

The concept, or even the existence, of *luck* is controversial. By its definition, luck would seem to be a chance occurrence—one that brings good or bad fortune to an individual. Is luck really the metaphorically *accidental* occurrence that favors some but has no assignable cause?

Luck is a part of many stories about creative outcomes. Alexander Fleming reportedly went on vacation and returned to discover mold growing in his Petrie dish. Examination of the mold in the cast-off dish led to the development of penicillin.

Goodyear's discovery of vulcanized rubber also has elements of luck involved. When Goodyear accidently spilled India rubber and sulfur onto a hot stove, he discovered that the rubber became more durable and could be of practical use in various products. He called his process vulcanization.

The development of Post-it Notes also involved some chance—actually, two aspects of what might be called luck. Spencer Silver, who was working for the 3M research laboratories, inadvertently developed the adhesive. He was looking for a strong bonding agent, but finding only a weak adhesive, he put the project aside. However, 4 years later, another researcher from the same lab, Arthur Fry, discovered a need for Silver's weak adhesive. He wanted to mark several pages in his choir hymnal. When individual pieces of paper kept falling out of the book, he recalled Silver's work and recognized that the weak adhesive could solve his problem. Ten years after the original discovery of the weak adhesive, 3M started marketing Post-it Notes. Was luck involved here?

In his bestselling book, *Thinking Fast and Slow*, Kahneman contends that luck is an important aspect of every success story.[15] He points out that there is almost always an

---

[15] D. Kahneman, *Thinking Fast and Slow* (New York, NY: Farrar, Strauss, & Giroux, 2011).

element of luck that changes a mediocre outcome into a notable triumph. Additionally, if luck is a determinant of creativity, Kahneman suggests that there is a question of how much credit one can take for any outcome.

Louis Pasteur (chemist, scientist, and inventor) speaks of "chance as favoring the prepared mind."[16] This famous quote suggests that luck plays a role in creative outcomes, but also acknowledges that the creator must have a mind prepared to discover something new. Studying and analyzing a field is the best way to prepare the mind for the development of creative outcomes.

Brian Tracy (motivational speaker and author; born 1944) agrees with Pasteur's approach. However, he goes a step further, proposing that luck is quite predictable and requires an individual to be open to possibility. "If you want more luck, take more chances. Be more active. Show up more often."[17]

So who explains the concept of luck most accurately: Kahneman, Pasteur, or Tracy? How does luck relate to creativity? Perhaps it doesn't really matter as long as individuals are able to recognize the dynamic aspects of a situation that chance places before them as they seek creative outcomes.

---

[16] L. Pasteur and J. Lister, *Collected Writings* (New York, NY: Kaplan, 2008), v.

[17] B. Tracy, *No Excuses!: The Power of Self-Discipline for Success in Your Life* (Boston, MA: DeCapo Press, 2014).

CHAPTER THREE

INTELLIGENCE, CRITICAL THINKING,
KNOWLEDGE AND LEARNING

Individuals must activate their cognitive abilities to develop creative outcomes. In this chapter, the discussion centers on how intelligence, critical thinking, knowledge, and learning influence creativity.

Intelligence

Logically, intelligence must factor into the development of creative outcomes. The MacArthur Fellows interviewed for the dissertation agree that intelligence is a factor, but they are also certain that their creative success does not depend on having an extremely high IQ. Indeed, they refute the idea that the prestigious MacArthur award, which is nicknamed the *genius award*, is related to any definition of genius. Not one of the fellows interviewed claims to have an extraordinarily high IQ, but, rather, they attribute any creative ability to various personal characteristics and habits, as well as precise approaches to creative efforts. Specifically, the MacArthur Fellows laud the value of intense work, logical analysis, and critical thinking that they believe will, in the course of a lifetime, produce more accomplishments.

When talking about high IQ and its relationship to genius, Dr. Saul Griffith (MacArthur Fellow: Class of 2007) says it best. "I really don't think that there are any geniuses. I just think that there are people who work hard and rigorously; if you work hard and rigorously, you will be perceived as a genius."

Saul is certainly very accomplished, and some people might consider him a genius based on his advancements in robotics, solar power, wind power, and the storage of natural gas for use in automobiles. He received a Ph.D. from the Massachusetts Institute of Technology (MIT) for his work in programmable assembly and self-replicating machines and has been awarded multiple patents in textiles, optics, nanotechnology, and energy production. This prolific inventor is the founder and current CEO of Otherlab, which is headquartered in the Mission District of San Francisco.

Eminent researcher and MacArthur Fellow from the Class of 1981, Howard Gardner, supports Saul's claim that creativity is not associated with an extremely high IQ—certainly not an IQ that is measured in the genius range.[18] Rather, Gardner recognizes that many creative people are intelligent (have an above average IQ), but an extremely high IQ does not guarantee creativity.[19]

Since IQ tests measure intelligence and do not measure creative potential, there is not any established relationship between IQ and creativity. Therefore, individuals who score in

---

[18] Mensa International, a society of individuals with high IQs, claims that genius requires an IQ in the upper 2% on any approved intelligence test.

[19] H. Gardner, *Creating Minds* (New York, NY: Basic Books, 1993).

the genius range on standardized intelligence tests do not necessarily demonstrate a propensity for creative thinking. Additionally, individuals who receive high scores on intelligence tests demonstrate that they know the conventional answer that is expected on a standardized test. Conventional answers are not the norm in the realm of creativity and individuals may actually impede their creative abilities when they accept the idea that there is always one *right* answer to any question.

Critical Thinking

Unlike a high IQ, critical thinking is imperative in creativity. Those who want to generate creative ideas and want to produce novel outcomes must exhibit good critical thinking skills.

Saul acknowledges that "thinking about thinking" is important. He has spent significant time over the past years reflecting on his reasoning processes with the goal of improving them. He says that a person needs to think rigorously to be successful. He admits that he often rails against weak thinking, so his self-analysis helps him examine the important rudiments of thought.

Critical thinking is important because it leads to an analytical examination of a situation, which can improve understanding of the boundaries and the overall nature of the circumstances involved. Such analytical thinking also becomes the basis for developing strategic approaches to a problem. Critical thinking is both the catalyst and methodology for various creative strategies. The bottom line is that creativity can emerge when thinking is precise and thorough and when a logical plan to search is developed. Also, the MacArthur Fellows interviewed point out that they gain insight by examining the creative processes they have used on past projects.

Cognitive Processes—Divergent and Convergent Thinking

Understanding the importance of creativity has led researchers to attempt to measure creative potential. To date, no definitive measurement of creative potential has been developed. Rather, a proxy for creative thought or potential has been proposed.

The proxy for creative thought is termed *divergent thinking*. Guilford first proposed divergent thinking as a measure of creativity, describing it as a cognitive process that emphasizes the importance of spontaneous and free-flowing thoughts.[20] Fluency, flexibility, redefinition, and originality are all manifestations of this distinctive thinking process. According to Guilford, fluency is an ability to generate multiple ideas that may aid in the search for a problem solution. Flexibility is related to categorical shifts in idea generation. Redefinition refers to the ability to relinquish old ways of construing familiar objects to use them for a new purpose. Originality is the ability to respond with unique or unusual answers. All four aspects of divergent thinking (fluency, flexibility, redefinition, and originality) are

---

[20] J. P. Guilford, "Creativity," *American Psychologist* 5, no. 9 (1950), 444-54.

helpful in producing creative ideas, but the problem is that individuals who score high on divergent thinking tests do not necessarily produce creative outcomes.

Convergent thinking is the opposite of divergent thinking. When employing convergent thinking, an individual brings together ideas and formulates a solution that can be implemented. Convergent thinking provides a way for individuals to distinguish a good idea from a bad idea or a creative possibility from a creative dead end.

Therefore, the best that can be said is that ideas from divergent thinking provide fuel for creative consideration, and convergent thinking can help evaluate the ideas and focus the process on a creative solution. However, divergent and convergent thinking do not guarantee creative results.

Ability to Understand Two Dimensions of Creativity

Saul distinguishes between two aspects of the creative process in his work. When a project is being imagined and conceived, Saul prefers a free-flowing environment—one that fosters examining new methodologies, testing the previously untested, and thinking largely outside of the scientific box. This part of Saul's laboratory has a definite ethos that encourages abstract and wide-range thinking that contributes to the success of the work product that is envisaged there. The workspace is casual in its layout and spirit. Groups working on different projects can co-mingle in various spaces, and these seemingly casual opportunities to convene contribute to the spirit of entrepreneurship.

There is, however, another side of Saul's laboratory. When systematic testing is needed to confirm ideas, the work is completed in a relatively bureaucratic and tightly organized environment where his employees are expected to be technically rigorous in the testing process. Concepts and designs are meticulously tested to make sure that products operate flawlessly. Here Saul counts on his engineers to be scientifically exact.

The more casual environment where abstract research is conducted and the rigor of the testing laboratory are sharply juxtaposed. In a sense, Saul employs *a science of discovery* in the innovative phases of a project—then he switches to a *science of verification* to prove his creative designs. In this way, he employs the best of his creative talents and the best of his scientific knowledge and expertise, combining them to innovate.

Saul's employees understand the different parts of the organization. They are comfortable with the division; however, a visitor, focusing on the more casual side of the business once commented that the workspace appears to have the atmosphere of an "adult Montessori." Using the word *playful* as a noun, Saul concurs that, at times, the staff participate in what he describes as "doing a lot of playful." While some may see this playful environment as a distraction to getting work accomplished, Saul understands that the atmosphere contributes to the creative outcomes.

Knowledge and Learning

According to the MacArthur Fellows interviewed, having basic knowledge of a subject is key to developing creative outcomes. In other words, an individual must understand the important corpus of knowledge that governs a specific field of expertise. Such expertise in a field is referred to as domain knowledge. This understanding is essential because, as Jim points out, no one can change the universal laws of the physical world.

However, accepted domain knowledge may extend beyond proven physical laws. In such cases, established domain knowledge may dampen creative efforts. If current perspectives in a field are over weighted or blindly accepted, creative alternatives may be missed. Therefore, it is necessary to have an open mind—one that is continually questioning current dogma.

The MacArthur Fellows interviewed also note the importance of continuing to learn, and they commonly seek knowledge in various fields. They emphasize the importance of ongoing learning because they understand creativity in terms of a directed, focused, and somewhat systematic process rather than one that is haphazard in nature. Hence, if creativity is a learned process, it is logical to invest in continuous learning that can lead to new ideas that may catalyze creative outcomes. Jim supports his personal commitment to continuous learning by reading numerous journals that help him expand his knowledge. He reads about new ideas in his field of primary expertise (engineering) and has extended his reading to all areas where his organization is active to expand his understanding of the current issues facing his company. Since Benetech involves itself in matters that impact the disabled community and is engaged with human rights issues, Jim reads extensively about these subjects.

The Role of Practice in Learning

According to a recent study, practice can improve performance; however, the effect of practice on performance varies with the domain.[21] According to the study, practice can improve results by 26% for games, 21% for music, 18% for sports, 4% for education, and 1% for professions.

Mastery based on practice seems logical. Technical skills mastery that can be acquired through practice is essential in many performance domains. However, practice alone does not guarantee skills enhancement. For instance, gains in music may also depend on a high quality of instruction and an individual's genetic makeup.

Popular author, Malcolm Gladwell, oversimplifies the concept of practice. He claims that 10,000 hours of practice in a subject will make an individual an expert in that area.[22] Gladwell's statement, however, is not supported by research and fails to take into consideration other personal characteristics and habits that can influence creativity.

---

[21] B. N. Macnamara, D. Z. Hambrick, and F. L. Oswald, "Deliberate Practice and Performance in Music, Games, Sports, Education, and Professions: A Meta-Analysis," *Psychological Science* August 25, no. 8 (2014): 1608-18.

[22] M. Gladwell, *Outliers: The Story of Success* (New York, NY: Little, Brown, 2008).

Learning by Error

The MacArthur Fellows interviewed also recognize that making errors should be expected and can advance creative efforts. Errors, in effect, are part of the search for creativity. The research participants, however, do not connect the concept of an error with failure; rather, they prefer to focus on the value of the learning that is associated with an error. Since learning from errors increases knowledge, errors should not inhibit further creative plans but rather should inform them.

Jim acknowledges the importance of learning from errors. Once he published a paper describing how a Benetech landmine elimination project had failed. According to Jim, the project was advanced with good intentions, but his organization had not realized the political ramifications of the plan. The project had to be abandoned because Jim's company failed to secure export permissions necessary for the landmine detection technology. In publishing the paper, Jim wanted his organization and others outside the organization to learn from the error. Perhaps Jim would agree with Henry David Thoreau who says, "If we will be quiet and ready enough, we shall find compensation in every disappointment."[23]

Saul also discusses how errors help him learn. He points out that when a person works at the edges of applied knowledge, it is necessary to accept the possibility that not all decisions will be correct. He even concedes, "I make more errors than most

---

[23] H. D. Thoreau and J. S. Cramer, *I to Myself: An Annotated Selection from the Journal of Henry D. Thoreau* (New Haven, CT: Yale University Press), 10.

people." The most important thing, he states, is to make errors quickly and then learn from them. In supervising projects, he is always determined to make decisions quickly to speed up the project, is good humored when he errs, and is determined to not be discouraged by his mistakes.

Being New to a Field Can Create Opportunity

Saul also suggests that creativity is likely to be enhanced when a person is new to a field. Excitement about learning is important in all situations, according to Saul, but he contends that the prospects of learning in a new domain have special merit and can yield exciting and novel results. This is because newcomers to a field are expected and encouraged to question the acknowledged subject experts and are more likely to ask probing questions that are not cynical and jaded. Such investigations can lead to new perceptions and discoveries.

The MacArthur Fellows interviewed generally agree that those who are new to the field may also not be aware of the entrenched assumptions and theories present in a domain and so may be more open to alternative concepts and approaches. Being able to think more broadly about an issue rather than accepting the status quo can free an individual to explore more widely.

However, neophytes who contest authority may also be viewed as coarse and tactless upstarts. Those with expert status in a domain may not appreciate the challenge from untested outsiders and may try to discount or even ridicule their ideas.

However, if a newcomer is able to persevere, novel ideas may influence current doctrine.

Moneyball, a popular movie produced in 2011, tells the story of Billy Beane, an untried General Manager for the Oakland Athletics, who puts his faith in an Ivy League economics student who claims to have a new system for assessing baseball players. Pushing aside the accepted way of assessing player talent, the duo use new and counterintuitive methods for player evaluation. The team manager and longtime team scouts are resistant to the new approach, but, as the team starts winning games, the skeptics realize the value of the new system. Beane's methods change the way baseball players are evaluated.

A main conclusion is that specialized knowledge is important in gaining domain expertise status. Additionally, learning does not conform to a timetable and depends on many factors. Finally, creativity favors those who remain eager to learn and have the mindset that additional exploration will yield exciting and creative outcomes.

CHAPTER FOUR

PITFALLS IN THE JOURNEY TO CREATIVITY

Individuals pursuing creative endeavors may be stalled or permanently thwarted by various conditions that obscure a complete understanding of a situation. In order to comprehend the essential elements in any circumstance, individuals involved must identify the nature and scope of the problem, fully grasp objectives, and successfully interpret ancillary information that is essential to the scenario. A successful creator will also sift through situational information looking for inconsistencies and will logically organize the information about the problem so that past assumptions can to be scrutinized and missing information identified. If an individual fails to consider important aspects of a situation or misinterprets facts, any solution that is uncovered may be compromised.

This chapter discusses some of the issues that can contribute to an inadequate understanding of a problem and hinder the development of a creative solution. Included are discussions concerning the limited usefulness of brainstorming by committee, the shortcomings of conventional wisdom, and the problems found when knowledge becomes entrenched.

Brainstorming

Brainstorming is a creative technique that was popularized by Alex Faickney Osborn.[24] This technique relies on groups of people to propose creative responses to issues and problems. The groups brainstorm to stimulate idea generation while suspending judgment on the concepts suggested. The rules of brainstorming are to (a) focus on quantity of ideas (the number of ideas and not the probability of their success), (b) withhold criticism of suggested ideas, and (c) welcome wild ideas that may spur creativity through association. Osborn suggests that brainstorming contributes to creative outcomes because assembled groups generate large numbers of ideas that have *ideative efficacy*.

Research, however, suggests that brainstorming is generally ineffective in creative problem solving.[25] Runco concludes that individuals are more likely to generate more and better ideas than groups. He explains this outcome in terms of *social loafing* among the participants. In effect, the idea of generating novel ideas is still important, but individuals, more so than groups, have a greater chance of producing creative alternatives.

The MacArthur Fellows generally agree with the shortcomings identified by Runco. While they don't entirely eschew group work to search for creative solutions, they agree

---

[24] A. F. Osborn, Applied Imagination: Principles and Procedures of Creative Thinking (New York, NY: Scribner, 1953).

[25] M. A. Runco, "Creativity," *Annual Review of Psychology* 55, no. 1 (2004): 657-687.

that creative brainstorming is overrated and that a group approach does not necessarily support the identification of creative outcomes. Rather the MacArthur Fellows have found success by better understanding a problem. They realize that gaining in-depth knowledge of a problem is critical. However, problem understanding is not a prerequisite or an outcome of brainstorming.

In his book, *The Wisdom of Crowds*, James Surowiecki suggests that groups of individuals have a special ability to make accurate judgments on a broad range of topics. At first glance, this suggestion seems to run counter to the experience of the MacArthur Fellows. However, noting that group intelligence has been scientifically demonstrated in a host of experiments, Surowiecki also states, "Groups are better at deciding between possible solutions to a problem than they are at coming up with them."[26]

Conventional Wisdom: Real Wisdom or Apocryphal

Conventional wisdom is the reliance on generally accepted ideas and opinions. This wisdom is not necessarily based on science, and its genesis may be folklore, stereotypes, sensationalized headlines, or poorly designed research that represents a lack of close scrutiny. Often, conventional wisdom involves shallow analysis or the acceptance of statements that

---

[26] J. Surowiecki, *The Wisdom of Crowds* (New York, NY: Doubleday, 2004), 60.

reflect a superficial interpretation of a complex phenomenon. Blind acceptance of conventional wisdom should be avoided.

Wilma Subra (MacArthur Fellow: Class of 1999) is a chemist by training and president of the Subra Company, a chemical laboratory and consulting firm in New Iberia, Louisiana. While she does have some paying customers in the area, 75% of Wilma's business is pro bono consulting. She has spent more than 3 decades providing technical assistance to citizens and communities who have been victimized by environmental polluters. She is a crusader who fights to stop corporations from polluting, and she also advocates for the cleanup of toxic waste sites. More often than not, citizen-led groups seek Wilma's help to fend off polluters. Clients are often from poor communities along the Mississippi River who could not possibly pay for her services. She is a community's last and best hope to stand up to the large corporate polluters that often seem oblivious or indifferent to the environmental disasters they create.

When community groups ask Wilma for help, she provides expertise in chemistry to help her clients understand the nature, source, and severity of the pollution. However, while Wilma supports local activist groups with her expertise and helps then consider options, she does not make decisions for the community. Rather, she seeks local leadership to spearhead the fight. She wants the community to take the lead and be vested in the struggle to protect and improve the local environment.

Wilma rejects conventional wisdom that suggests that individuals who are poor and do not have the benefit of a formal education will fail in a fight against corporate polluters. In addition, she rejects the idea that her clients are not capable of being effective leaders. Rather than assuming that the communities that she assists are not capable of representing themselves, Wilma encourages individuals to take leadership positions and fully participate in the dispute resolution. She is often content to watch individuals within the groups develop new leadership skills and competencies. She notes that more than one activist has run for elected office after participating in a fight against environmental polluters. Most importantly, Wilma celebrates when the faulty stereotypes of conventional wisdom are exposed.

In addition to the stereotypes that Wilma eschews in her work, life provides multiple other instances where conventional wisdom is a stumbling block in the search for creative solutions. In thinking about how conventional wisdom reveals itself in life, consider what often happens when someone asks why a procedure, process, or policy is pursued in a particular way. In other words, what happens when someone says, "Why do we do it this way?" The classic and often-heard statement to such a *why* question is *because we have always done it this way*. Consider this response as a cue to look more closely at the situation. A more in-depth analysis is needed because conventional wisdom can limit perspective. When additional viewpoints are considered, the range of alternative responses is increased and this can produce better alternatives and opportunities.

MacArthur Fellows interviewed concur with the idea that conventional wisdom is often faulty. They acknowledge that they are skeptical of such wisdom and are leery of accepting it without scrutiny. Saul's rejection of conventional wisdom is the most colorful. He describes conventional wisdom as "bullshit assumptions that are probably wrong."

Other individuals interviewed are not as lively in their disdain, but all share the same concern—that conventional wisdom is rarely scrutinized and leads to substandard analysis. The problem, according to the study participants, is that conventional wisdom is often the antithesis of research rigor and is akin to accepting facts based on faith rather than embracing empirical investigation and logic as virtuous and essential tenets of research.

One example of conventional wisdom concerns how much water an individual should drink. The conventional wisdom is that each person should drink eight glasses of water a day. [27] However, there is no consideration of a person's age, weight, or activity level—just the prescription to drink the approved amount. Looking into this health claim, it appears that the public has blindly accepted the recommendation of a dubious health expert who conducted no research to support his

---

[27] F. J. Stare and M. McWilliam, *Nutrition for Good Health* (Fullerton, CA: Plycon Press, 1974), 175.

claim.   Despite a lack of data on the subject, this 1974 prescription has persisted as conventional wisdom.

The point is that when any professed wisdom becomes generally accepted, but has not been scrutinized, it should be challenged because the consequences of blind acceptance may have a strong negative impact.   The following account comes from Elof Carlson, who documented the rise of eugenics as a pseudo-science.[28]

Eugenics—the study of how to improve the human species—became accepted doctrine during much of the 20th century.   Underlying the doctrine of eugenics is the belief that degeneracy is a medical problem that afflicts individuals.   This belief promotes the idea that individuals who have genetic defects or are presumed to have inherited undesirable traits should be prevented from procreating.

Eugenics implies that some individuals have little social worth.   Included in this reduced social worth category are people who are poor, people who exhibit diseases such as epilepsy or alcoholism, or people who are physically or mentally disadvantaged.   Degeneracy also includes those individuals thought to be unfit because they have inherited undesirable traits that lead them to be criminals or prostitutes.

Oscar McCulloch and David Starr Jordan promoted the eugenics doctrine and the compulsory sterilization of individuals who were deemed to be incorrigible degenerates.   McCulloch

---

[28] P. A. Lombardo, A. Logan, and M. J. Mehlman, *Century of Eugenics in America: From the Indiana Experiment to the Human Genome Era* (Bloomington, IN: Indiana University Press, 2011).

was a minister who led various Midwestern churches in the United States during his career. Jordan was a congregant at McCulloch's church and a biology professor at Indiana University. Jordan joined McCulloch in promoting eugenics. He claimed that eugenics was important because there was an obligation to cull the least productive individuals from society and to encourage the best and brightest to reproduce for the good of humankind. Later, Jordan became the inaugural president of Stanford University.

Dr. Harry Clay Sharp agreed that the genetic makeup of the human race could be improved by culling undesirables. While serving as an Indiana prison doctor, Sharp began advancing the goals of eugenics by performing vasectomies on prisoners deemed to be degenerate.

In 1907, the doctrine of eugenics was legitimized when the Indiana General Assembly passed legislation that allowed individuals deemed degenerate to be sterilized. The date of 1907 is important. For those readers who think that sterilizations based on the doctrine of eugenics began at the time that the Nazi regime was trying to purify humanity by eliminating the Jewish race, recognize that Hitler didn't become Chancellor of Germany until 1933. By 1933, compulsory sterilization was already well accepted in the United States. Eventually 30 states would legalize the procedure.

The eugenics movement was based on faulty logic. Eugenics claimed that genetic inheritance was responsible for what was considered to be antisocial behavior. In other words, eugenics promoted the concept that an individual's biology decided his or her life—in some cases dictating that an individual was inherently bad. This premise was accepted as conventional wisdom by the public in 1907 and was supported by a wide range of intellectuals, politicians, and community leaders.

Alexis Carrel, a French surgeon and biologist who received the 1912 Nobel Prize in medicine, supported the doctrine of eugenics and advocated for sterilization. Charles Lindberg was also a proponent. The American Public Health Association even supported eugenics by sponsoring an exhibition that toured the United States from 1934 to 1943.

This example of the acceptance of conventional wisdom should be a warning. Conventional wisdom has the potential to be dangerous, spreading inaccurate information validated by unsound research. Regrettably, when unchallenged, not only does the public accept conventional wisdom, but it can also become institutionalized in society through legislation. Once established as law, conventional wisdom is difficult to challenge.

While eugenics is not a currently accepted theory and compulsory sterilization does not represent current therapy, the conventional wisdom surrounding the goals and processes of eugenics has not been entirely debunked. Some scientists involved in the Human Genome Project, an international scientific research project conducted between 1990 and 2003, still consider some genetic combinations to be better than others, and they still seek ways to alter human DNA to improve human genetics. Surely, societal goals are more humane now—or is this a new sort of conventional wisdom?

Entrenchment of Knowledge

The concept of entrenched knowledge is related to conventional wisdom, and, in some cases, it too can inhibit creativity because it is another form of false wisdom. Generally, the entrenchment of knowledge refers to an adherence to traditional methods and approaches that have gained widespread acceptance within a field of study.

Dr. Victoria Hale (MacArthur Fellow: Class of 2006) discusses her experience with entrenched knowledge. The story begins with Victoria's dream to live in a world where all people have their basic needs met. In particular, she wants more equity in the availability of health resources and to make sure that those who are "voiceless and invisible" can avail themselves of modern medical solutions. Fortunately, Victoria has positioned herself to help the world's poorest attain better medical care. She received a Ph.D. in pharmaceutical chemistry and is a social entrepreneur in the pharmaceutical industry where she develops new drugs and medical solutions.

As Victoria considered how she could help the poorest of the world get the medical attention that they require and deserve, she recognized that the for-profit model that generally requires a solitary pursuit of profit was simply not an effective way to approach the problem. As a result, Victoria first created a nonprofit pharmaceutical organization. However, over time,

Victoria realized that this model could not support the sweeping goals that she wanted to pursue to solve the health problems of the poor. While the nonprofit financial model was sufficient to support nonprofit research and the creation of drugs, it did not allow Victoria's organization to achieve the broader and more impactful goal of reaching actual patients.

Acknowledging the shortcomings of the nonprofit model, Victoria began her search for a new hybrid business model that would promote her goals. She considered the possibility of seeking an advanced degree in business (MBA) to increase her understanding of the central theories of commerce. When she consulted others for advice, they dissuaded her from embracing a traditional business curriculum because such an education would be counterproductive; mentors told her, "You will be convinced that your ideas will never work."

Victoria did not go to business school and did not learn about traditional business models. However, she did create a new and innovative hybrid business arrangement. Working within the new structure, Victoria developed an effective, reversible, and long-acting IUD birth control device. She then partnered with a well-respected for-profit business partner that licensed the products for sale in the lucrative U.S. market. By securing an ongoing revenue stream (in the form of an established royalty) and the support of her partner in distributing the medical devices around the world, Victoria now has the means to fund future drug development and achieve her social justice goals of providing health resources to the poor around the world.

Victoria's story brings home the point that, in some cases, formalized education may support entrenched knowledge and discourage alternative approaches to a problem. Victoria is not alone in her rejection of traditional education to solve a complex problem. Research studies by Teresa Amabile indicate that while formal education can encourage creativity, "an excessively extended formal education might be detrimental because of an over-reliance on established algorithms or a slavish imitation of models."[29]

Entrenchment also occurs when domain experts control a field or subject. As authorities in a particular realm, these individuals believe they understand all there is to know about a topic, and they are invested in the status quo. Fearing that a change in established doctrine may involve losing face and expert status, reigning experts may not be willing to admit that current assumptions and theories have been superseded by more up-to-date ideas and hypotheses. According to Thomas Kuhn (American physicist, historian, and philosopher of science; 1922-1996), new approaches are generally shunned until current experts retire or die.[30]

Saul discusses his experience with the jaded experts who fail to see possibilities because of their entrenchment in current

---

[29] T. M. Amabile, *The Social Psychology of Creativity* (New York, NY: Springer-Verlag, 1983), 197.

[30] T. S. Kuhn, *The Structure of Scientific Revolutions* (Chicago, IL: University of Chicago Press, 2012).

theory. He notes that such experts can end up asking the wrong questions about a subject or be duped into accepting a faulty premise or imprecise test results. As a result, they fail to experiment with unconventional hypotheses that might provide alternative, potentially creative solutions.

A good example of entrenched knowledge comes from the field of economics. For decades, economists claimed that humans always act in their own best interest, consistently choosing to maximize value in their decisions. Herbert Simon disputed this claim and proposed an alternate theory—the theory of bounded rationality.[31] This theory claims that humans are not always rational in their decision making because they are constrained by their limited cognitive ability and the finite information they have available to make decisions. Despite numerous studies that demonstrate that humans are boundedly rational, some economists still clung to the notion of human rationality. Even when Simon was awarded the 1978 Nobel Prize in Economics for his work, some researchers were still skeptical. Ironically, the scientists who refused to accept the scientific evidence were demonstrating the point that humans are not always rational. The lesson is that any type of knowledge should be thoroughly scrutinized before it is accepted as truth.

Scientists are currently testing their knowledge about the standardized treatment of cancer. Oncologists, who for decades have prescribed chemotherapy and radiation for treatment of

---

[31] K. M. Eisenhardt and M. J. Zbaracki, "Strategic Decision Making," *Strategic Management Journal* 13 (1992): 17-37.

cancerous tumors, now have empirical evidence that another form of treatment, *gene therapy*, may provide better results for the suppression of cancer in some cases.

The development of gene therapy means that oncologists are now confronted with multiple therapies that can potentially help patients with cancer. The question remains: Will traditional cancer experts accept gene therapy as a legitimate contender in the cancer-fighting arena or will they remain dedicated to supporting only traditional cancer treatments?

Entrenchment of knowledge can take various alternate forms. Innovator's dilemma, flawed belief systems, spot blindness, and compartmentalized knowledge are all forms of knowledge entrenchment that can cause a failure to accurately understand a situation and can inhibit creativity. Discussion on these subjects follows.

Innovator's Dilemma

Clayton Christensen introduced the term *innovator's dilemma*.[32] The term refers to a condition where successful entrepreneurs are so connected to their ideas that they fail to see or act on new opportunities because they do not want to move on from their initial concepts or designs. Citing economic interest as a factor that may impair clear analysis of situations, Christensen notes that this shortsightedness can keep ostensibly creative people from continuing to innovate in a field.

---

[32] C. M. Christensen, *The Innovator's Dilemma: When New Technologies Cause Great Firms to Fail* (Boston, MA: Harvard Business School Press, 1997).

The history of Kodak is an example of how innovator's dilemma impacted the future of a once great company. Kodak, or the Eastman Kodak Company, as it was formerly known, marketed its first camera in 1888. The company became an icon in the camera and film industry. It continued to advance technology and market products in cameras, film, and film processing.

In 1975, Kodak invented the first digital camera. However, the company failed to capitalize on the technology, fearing that the new technology, which did not use traditional film, would cannibalize its traditional chemical-based film and paper business. So while Kodak presided over the technical breakthrough of digital photography, the leadership of the organization decided that the company should *play it safe* and not jeopardize current profits. Ultimately, this strategy proved disastrous, as Kodak filed for bankruptcy protection in 2012. In 2013, Kodak emerged from bankruptcy, but it remains a shadow of its former self. By denying the inevitability of digital processes and remaining entrenched in earlier technologies, the company made a grievous error that forestalled future *Kodak Moments*.

In the dissertation study, when Jim discussed innovator's dilemma, he noted that it is a common and potentially destructive condition for organizations that have developed specialized knowledge. Wanting to avoid the pitfalls of remaining committed to a particular technology that has become outdated, Jim recommends that, like Benetech, organizations should routinely develop a *market exit strategy* for each product. In this way, a company can prevent innovator's dilemma by being ready to move on from obsolete approaches.

Flawed Belief Systems

A conventional aphorism is: "I'll believe it when I see it." Perhaps a better expression would be: "I'll see it when I believe it." The following examples describe how faulty beliefs can obstruct thinking and action—impacting human advancement.

In 1954, Roger Bannister broke the world record for the mile. Until that time, medical professionals believed that human physiology would not allow humans to run a sub-4-minute mile. Bannister, a medical student, was a non-believer. Since he did not accept the entrenched belief held by the medical profession, he set out to prove the experts wrong. Moreover, when he did break the barrier, Bannister not only proved that the belief was faulty, but he also allowed others to dismiss the artificial absolute in human physiology—ushering in many new records on the track. In fact, Bannister only held the world record for 6 weeks. Additionally, 10 years after Bannister exploded the myth of the mile, runners in elite competitions could not expect better than an eighth-place finish when completing a 4-minute mile. By raising their sights and dismissing the idea that humans had a maximum speed, top runners reset their goals and adapted their training to accomplish what was formerly *impossible*.

In 1954 at the Commonwealth Games in Vancouver, Canada, another runner demonstrated the pitfalls of entrenched knowledge. Coming into the stadium for the finish of the marathon competition, Jim Peters had a 17-minute lead. It was a hot day and Peters was clearly suffering and delirious. He fell unconscious 220 yards short of the finish line. In that year, there was little water available on the marathon course, and there were rules against taking drinks in the first 10 miles. Moreover, Peters believed that any liquid intake on the day of the race was harmful to performance. Instead of water, Peters ingested salt tablets. This prohibition against hydration seems ludicrous today, but the flawed belief of 1954 kept Peters from properly replenishing his body with liquids. Fortunately, it didn't cost him his life.

In light of present-day understanding of physiology, these two examples seem hard to believe. However, is it possible that there are other assumptions that the public currently accepts that are just as unreasonable?

Spot Blindness

Entrenched knowledge also limits creativity by potentially creating spot blindness. Such blindness occurs when an individual accepts a simplified or distorted representation of a situation or fails to see the crucial boundaries of an issue.

To allow creativity to emerge, it is important to be able to overcome spot blindness by recognizing functional fictions that have been embraced—consciously or unconsciously. What invalid assumptions should be discarded? What shortcuts in thinking must be corrected to overcome incomplete or erroneous suppositions?

The history of the development of the compact disc (CD) provides an example of spot blindness. The story involves the partnership between two formidable companies of the 1970s—Philips and Sony. These companies pioneered the technology to store digital audio. The CD, unveiled to the world in 1979, used laser technology to read information stored on a disc without any physical contact with that disc.

How does this work relate to spot blindness? According to company history, the Philips engineers first created what was termed the ALP (audio long play). Given that the ALP was to compete with vinyl records, the engineers created a disc that was 20 centimeters (7.87 inches) in diameter—roughly equal to the standard diameter of vinyl records that were distributed at the time. The idea that the new technology CDs should replicate the size of the vinyl records initially went untested. Fortunately, Lou Otters, the technical director of the audio division at Philips, recognized that the physical size of the CD should be questioned. He suggested that the CD should be made smaller than the dominant vinyl dimensions, having the goal to hold about one hour of music and still be readily portable.

The partnership between Philips and Sony ultimately produced a CD format that could contain as much as 74 minutes of music. The rumor was that a CD that held 74 minutes of music could play, without interruption, a full-length version of Beethoven's Ninth Symphony. While this story may be fictional, the idea is intriguing. The most compelling result of the standardized CD format was that it produced a physical disc that was only 4.5 inches in diameter. This size factor significantly increased portability and prompted the creation of portable CD players. Moreover, the CD technology removed the need to flip to a second side of a record or tape, and the listener could search for individual songs that could be immediately played.

While music listening has progressed since the development of the CD, this example points out how spot blindness can hamper efforts to see creative solutions. Sir Karl Popper, philosopher and professor, expresses this point succinctly: "We approach everything in the light of a preconceived theory. This being the case, we must make sure that our preconceptions are not faulty or incomplete."[33]

Compartmentalized Knowledge

In the dissertation research, Saul discusses how domain knowledge that is too fragmented can hinder scientific study. He notes that experts in a field can become too compartmentalized in their knowledge. According to Saul, the disciplines of biology, chemistry, and physics are now segmented to the point that expertise is very narrow. This, he feels, inhibits creativity because scientists are no longer able to understand the broader picture, and they have trouble speaking to each other because they don't share the same basis of understanding or vocabulary. In his own work, Saul prefers to think of himself as a natural philosopher who understands and applies scientific

---

[33] K. R. Popper, "Normal Science and Its Dangers," in *Criticism and the Growth of Knowledge*, ed. I. Lakatos and A. Musgrave (London: Cambridge University Press), 52.

concepts from all three fields—biology, chemistry, and physics. To preserve his broader scope of understanding, Saul is committed to continuing his education in subfields within each discipline with the intention of reducing the occurrence of compartmentalized knowledge. Experts in other fields may find this suggestion helpful as they review the breadth of their expertise and consider future study.

The goal of this chapter has been to introduce the reader to potential pitfalls and downsides to commonly accepted aspects of creative outcome generation. Those who seek creative outcomes need to be aware of the inherent drawbacks in these issues and avoid simply accepting them as reliable creative approaches.

CHAPTER FIVE

CHARACTERISTICS AND HABITS THAT
SUPPORT CREATIVITY

Creative individuals are often described as having a sense of purpose. This sense of purpose is a drive that can be characterized as an intentionality that involves deliberate and calculated attempts to find novel solutions through focus on stated goals. In turn, specific personal characteristics and habits support this focus. This chapter discusses characteristics and habits that the dissertation interviewees identified as important to their creative work.

A characteristic may be defined as a distinguishing feature, quality, or property. However, a characteristic is not thought to be genetically determined. This means that creativity can be nurtured. Habits are related to characteristics in the sense that they represent behavior patterns that are acquired through frequent repetition. Habits may also be cultivated.

The MacArthur Fellows of the research project all acknowledge that their personal characteristics and habits reinforce their creative potential. Following are the personal attributes that the fellows most often discussed: passion for the work, curiosity and openness to new experiences, risk taking, responding to failure, persistence, and action.

Passion for the Work

All of the MacArthur Fellows interviewed concede that loving what they do makes work exciting. They emphasize the idea that seeking creative outcomes is inspiring, satisfying, and just plain fun. Passion translates into pleasure in the workspace and produces energy to pursue creative activities. Additionally, passion promotes devotion to creative goals.

Saul, characteristically blunt, addresses the nature of passion. He says, "I am passionate about everything that I do so . . . I don't do anything half-assed." He continues with career advice concerning passion, saying, "I don't believe anyone can do anything that they are not passionate about. When we hire people, we show them all of the things we are doing and I tend to say—which of these things ignites [your] passion, and I encourage them to work on that and not work on something that they don't feel like doing."

Dr. Wes Jackson (MacArthur Fellow: Class of 1992) speaks about how his passion for improving the planet's environmental health inspired him to establish The Land Institute. This institute, founded in 1976, recognizes the long-term negative environmental effects of traditional farming where regular tilling causes soil erosion and overall soil degradation. The mission of The Land Institute is to encourage farmers around the world to support sustainable farming methods by establishing Natural Systems Agriculture.

Natural Systems Agriculture is a fundamentally different way to produce food that is more sustainable and takes advantage of natural efficiencies available in nature. This kind of agriculture focuses on the cultivation of various types of perennial crops that are planted in the same field. Wes calls this approach "perennial polyculture cropping." It drastically reduces the need to annually till and replant fields. Additionally, the combination of plant species in a field mimics the vegetation of the natural and healthy prairie ecosystem.

The fact that Wes has sustained his commitment to the work of The Land Institute since 1976 is a tribute to his passion for the mission of the nonprofit. Also, Wes has a unique understanding of the relationship between passion and reason. He says, "Passion without reason is hysterical. Reason without passion is sterile." This memorable adage has defined Wes' life, and he cannot and does not want to separate passion and reason. His passion for making agriculture more sustainable, coupled with reason, undergirds his creativity.

When Jim discusses his emotional attachment to the work that he does, he begins by saying that, generally, scientists do not have a reputation for being demonstrative about the projects they pursue. However, despite his pragmatic scientific background, passion spurs his efforts. Jim's passion is expressed when he develops technological solutions for social problems. Jim points out, "It's about making a difference . . . about solving problems . . . [and] the most exciting, juicy problems that I can imagine are social problems."

Victoria describes the passion that she feels for her work as *a calling*. She understands this calling to be an imperative to pursue work with and for the poor. In speaking about her work, Victoria identifies two ways that passion motivates her. First, she points out that anger or frustration can manifest itself as passion. Such passion helps her concentrate her energy on an idea or project, helping her to intensely focus on a task. She does not deny that these negative emotions can arouse her to action, but she notes that over the long term they are not sufficient motivation to accomplish a project.

What is really needed to sustain activity and complete goals is a second dimension of passion. Victoria describes this dimension as the ability to "roll with the current." If a person can do this, his or her passion may be put to better use and more can be accomplished than through actions fueled by anger. The passion arising from anger or frustration is like a fire that burns hot and quickly, but the passion that is associated with thoughtful determination may give off less initial heat but burns longer. According to Victoria, it is this second type of passion that sustains concerted efforts that support creative activities.

The idea that creative individuals are likely to be passionate about their work is not a new concept. Lubart notes that creative people are generally intrinsically motivated. When so motivated, individuals find joy, satisfaction, and positive challenge in their work, and the desire to be creative is not enhanced by the lure of monetary gains.[34]

---

[34] T. I. Lubart, "Creativity" in *Thinking and Problem Solving*, 2nd ed., ed. R. J. Sternberg (San Diego CA: Academic Press, 1994), 289-332.

Curiosity and Openness to New Experiences

For study participants, curiosity is a catalyst for their creativity. Each interviewee has cultivated an interest in a subject or domain simply because the field is interesting and warrants more investigation. In other words, creativity is spurred by an interest in knowledge for its own sake. Some of the MacArthur Fellows describe their curiosity as a quality that they associate with young children. They note that the curiosity of a child, like their own, is unbounded and encourages new experiences just for the sake of doing and being.

Saul wants to hire individuals who like to indulge their curiosity and who desire to solve problems that they find interesting. To support his employees, he provides a work environment that encourages inquisitiveness. In Saul's estimation, work judiciously mixed with play supports and encourages curiosity, so it is not surprising that Saul's lab has been characterized as an adult Montessori where his researchers can express their child-like curiosity in a playful atmosphere.

Victoria considers the natural way that children pursue their curiosity. She discusses how children's curiosity encourages them to easily believe in themselves and express themselves without embarrassment. Victoria also notes that later in life self-doubt may begin to plague individuals and restrict their self-expression. Victoria, by her own assessment, continues to express her curiosity even into adulthood.

Gardner points out that Albert Einstein continued to think about issues like a child throughout his life,[35] and I. I. Rabi, another redoubtable physicist, once declared, "I think that physicists are the Peter Pans of the human race. They never grow up and they keep their curiosity. Once you are sophisticated, you know too much—far too much."[36]

In addition to being curious, the MacArthur Fellows are open to new experiences. Being open means that an individual maintains an expansive mindset that is always ready to engage new and interesting situations. Such openness reinforces a *search* for thought-provoking problems that pique curiosity. Being open also allows the mind to massage, connect, and interchange thoughts and ideas that can lead to discovery—discovery of new facts, new patterns, and new relationships.

Regrettably, family, school, and community influences may adversely affect curiosity and openness. Pressure to conform to societal expectations by getting the *right answer* can discourage and inhibit curiosity. Additionally, the negative effects of media that bombard the public with pessimistic evidence of human failures can have a dulling influence on curiosity and openness.

Risk Taking

Sternberg, an eminent researcher in creativity, recognizes that creative people are likely to take some risks in their search

---

[35] H. Gardner, *Creating Minds* (New York, NY: Basic Books, 1993), 89-90.

[36] Ibid.

for creative solutions.[37] Creative people, his data suggest, exhibit a sensible level of risk taking that is termed *calculated*. The term associates a certain course of action with alternatives that have been given full consideration and where potential gain is greater than any potential harm that might occur.

The MacArthur Fellows interviewed unanimously agree that their calculated risk taking is an important element of the creative process and is essential in completing innovative projects. They conclude that whenever new ideas are advanced, there is some risk.

When Jim talks about his calculated risk taking, he acknowledges that he considers the risk factors and is willing to support a project: "Stick with it past the difficulties, but not hold on to something that's obviously going to sink." Jim also promotes risk-taking actions in his managers. He points out that staff errors generally don't result in firing because in an innovative organization dismissing someone for taking a calculated risk that doesn't pay off would "kill our culture." The normal remedy for such errors, according to Jim, is to stop the process, learn from the error, try something different, and move forward with the project.

Saul is satisfied with his willingness to take calculated risks both personally and in the companies he has founded. For example, his organization's work on solar cell control required developmental research in bellows design. Overcoming the

---

[37] R. J. Sternberg, "The Nature of Creativity," *Creativity Research Journal* 18, no. 1 (2006): 87-98.

reticence and disagreement of five Ph.D. designers, Saul allowed a young intern to experiment with a new concept in design. The risk taking paid off when the intern's design worked. Saul was satisfied that, despite the objections of others and some misgivings of his own, he gave the go-ahead to spend money and use the intern's time to examine the idea.

Aaron Dworkin (MacArthur Fellow: Class of 2005) has had extensive training in violin performance. He could have made a living as a full-time performing artist, but he preferred to redirect his talents to creating a nonprofit arts organization that focuses on youth development and works to increase racial diversity in classical music performance. The Sphinx Organization, the nonprofit that he founded, has become a leading national arts organization that continues to transform lives through the power of diversity and the arts.

The genesis of Aaron's interest in music was seeing and hearing his adopted mother play the violin. She inspired his love of music, in general, and his affinity for the violin, in particular. As a young music student, Aaron noticed that he was the only person of color in his music classes and, at times, seemingly, the only biracial audience member at concerts. Realizing that minority musicians were uncommon in classical musical circles, he pondered how he might introduce the pleasure of such music to all races. He also wanted to find a way to help young minority students learn how to play instruments so that they could increase their chances of establishing careers in classical music performance.

As Aaron discusses how the Sphinx Organization has influenced his life, he notes risk taking is an important factor in his success. He summarizes his feelings on risk taking by saying, "A lot of the work that we do requires the risk of doing something that hasn't been done before." Recognizing the inherent risk of doing something for the first time, Aaron speaks of the need to have courage in pressing forward. He also points out another factor associated with risk. He acknowledges that completing a project successfully (when there is significant risk) can result in considerable personal satisfaction.

Victoria prefers to describe her risk taking in terms of a simile. For her, learning to take risks is like flying on a trapeze. The trapeze artist must swing from bar to bar and can only transfer from one swing to another by letting go of the first swing before the second trapeze is within reach. Hence, a person needs to trust that he or she can survive in the "space between the trapeze bars" where one is literally falling. According to Victoria, the important lesson is that you can survive the risk, but you must have the courage to take action. Although the veritable leap of faith can feel like quicksand for a period of time, Victoria believes that this place of risk is "where you really shine and where a growth opportunity is."

Edward Jenner, a pioneer in the use of vaccines, believed that a vaccine could reduce the incidence of the deadly smallpox disease. He was willing to experiment with his vaccine on children—including his 11-month-old son. His willingness to take a risk resulted in a reduction in the death rate from smallpox and an increased interest in vaccines to prevent other diseases. Using his son as an early subject was both courageous and audacious—a risk with potential serious and very personal consequences.

Susan Sygall (MacArthur Fellow: Class of 2000) is also willing to take risks to fulfill her mission as an international human rights advocate. In 1981, Susan co-founded Mobility International USA (MIUSA). The mission of MIUSA is to empower people around the world who have disabilities. The mission is accomplished by advocating for human rights and by promoting the inclusion of people with disabilities in international exchange and international development.[38]

MIUSA provides specific information to businesses and organizations on how to increase disability inclusion in such activities as study abroad, international volunteer teaching, and work exchange programs. In this way, Susan works to make sure that individuals with disabilities have opportunities to participate in international exchange and development programs—programs that have not traditionally sought out participants with disabilities.

The mission of the organization is personal to Susan. After an automobile accident, she became a wheelchair user. However, rather than focus her life as one constrained and

---

[38] International exchange refers to intercultural exchange, such as college study abroad programs. International development refers to foreign assistance provided to developing countries for building the capacity needed to implement sustainable solutions to problems.

framed by disability, Susan sets her professional and personal goals based on her abilities and vision for her life.

Susan points out that, sometimes, individuals with disabilities are unwilling to take even calculated risks because they are constrained by what she calls deficit thinking. According to Susan, deficit thinking is triggered when individuals perceive that being a member of a group with specific characteristics (e.g., a physical disability) will have outcomes and experiences that are always negative. In other words, deficit thinking promotes a belief that success is not available to an individual because personal circumstances will dictate continuing failure.

A personal story about Susan demonstrates that she is not prone to deficit thinking. While in college, and after her disabling automobile accident, Susan decided to study abroad. Rather than believing that her disability should narrow her educational opportunities, Susan chose to expand her experiences by accepting a Rotarian scholarship for study in Australia. Not only was she adventuresome enough to travel to Australia, she also flew to New Zealand where she and a friend, like many other young tourists in the 1970s, hitchhiked around the country. Susan's friend also used a wheelchair; consequently, they were two young travelers in wheelchairs, hitchhiking together in New Zealand. According to Susan, it was an experience of a lifetime, but Susan, in describing the trip, focused on the great adventure, seen through the eyes of two young people, and simply dismissed the disability part.

Deficit thinking can damage self-perceptions and prevent individuals from moving forward successfully. Moreover, deficit thinking may discourage individuals from taking even minor risks because they believe that their life circumstances will contribute to a self-fulfilling prophecy. Therefore, those who experience this sort of thinking will not likely be creative unless they can overcome the notion that they are destined to fail.

Susan's answer to the problem of deficit thinking for those with disabilities is to promote what she describes as *infiltration*. Infiltration is Susan's word for a kind of advocacy that encourages individuals with disabilities to bring themselves and others with disabilities directly into existing programs. An interesting by-product of infiltration is that it requires people with disabilities to push beyond preconceived notions that fuel deficit thinking. Ultimately, Susan believes that infiltration can activate *chutzpah* to promote goals and self-esteem and reverse deficit thinking.

While all of the MacArthur Fellows interviewed assert that risk taking is an important element in creativity, they also recognize that when individuals take risks, they don't always succeed. This truth leads to another important characteristic necessary to creativity—a realistic and practical view of failure. Those who seek creative outcomes must develop a way to deal with failure.

Responding to Failure

The MacArthur Fellows share their concern that sometimes a fear of failure threatens creativity. Not only can such fear inhibit risk taking, but it can also poison nascent creative efforts. However, a fear of failure can occasionally invade the personal thoughts of even the most assured. In discussing the dangers of giving into a fear of failure, the MacArthur Fellows point to strategies that they have developed to overcome fear.

Project Failure or Personal Failure

The first point that the MacArthur Fellows make is that there is a difference between a project failing and an individual failing. Study participants point to their belief that while society may judge an outcome as a failure, the individuals associated with the project do not, by association, become failures. In other words, the MacArthur Fellows interviewed do not consider a project failure a personal catastrophe.

When Victoria considers how she avoids fear and self-doubt, she returns to the trapeze simile and likens a fear of failure to thoughts that might be experienced by a trapeze artist. Victoria proposes that the trapeze artist may have some fear and that, at times, fear might serve a good purpose in keeping a person alive, but, ultimately, being paralyzed with fear will not get the job done. Therefore, with or without action, the result is the same. A project can fail based on actions taken or not taken.

The MacArthur Fellows interviewed recognize that a failure to act is the ultimate weakness. Aaron articulates this point precisely. He notes, "Tons of projects fail and initiatives fail," but "people fail when they fail to act." The bottom line is that the MacArthur Fellows have fears, but they overcome their qualms and self-doubt in order to act.

Reframing the Concept of Failure

Interviewees note that when facing evidence of a project failure, they are often able to reframe events and recast a weakening project that is off course into one that is still viable. Some interviewees even use similar phrasing to describe such situations. When considering an assignment that is stalled or in danger of failing, they speak of the project problems as *bumps in the road*.

The key to the reframing strategy is that the MacArthur Fellows do not consider these bumps as markers of failure. Rather, they take such occurrences in stride and do not respond to challenges by invoking a vision of failure. Instead, to them, a bump in the road is a temporary anomaly that needs to be addressed before more action is taken. This reframing of what others might consider failure allows the study participants to maintain a positive outlook and a willingness to continue. Moreover, the interviewees also assume that because they are doing something challenging, bumps in the road should be expected. The interviewees display a notable resilience that protects them from being overcome by a sense of failure.

The Discouraging Words of Others

When outsiders or insiders discount work or presume future failure, individuals may succumb to a growing sense of impending disaster. Although others may be projecting their own feelings of doubt, discouraging words have the potential to reduce confidence and impede action. The MacArthur Fellows, however, describe a way of counteracting the naysayers of the world. They take words of criticism as a challenge.

Saul has his share of critics. His inventions have been scrutinized in the press. With the media expressing disdain or outright contempt concerning some of his efforts, he has repeatedly rebounded from the discouraging words to continue his efforts. In responding to criticisms, Saul resists the desire to engage in a war of words with cynics or to be overwhelmed by the negativism generated. He, instead, sets aside his personal reaction to others and depends on scientific rigor and predictive tests to support his theories, recognizing that empirical evidence provides the ultimate proof in the world of science.

Victoria recognizes that those who criticize her ideas may actually galvanize her resolve and energize her actions. Criticism, she notes, may actually help advance her work. When traditional business experts discounted the feasibility of a hybrid business model that included a nontraditional drug development program, Victoria, rather than being dissuaded by the naysayers, preferred to test her innovative model in the laboratory of capitalistic business.

This ability to ignore skeptics may be associated with self-assurance or self-worth characteristics or may just signal a propensity to be thick-skinned. Saul and Victoria, however, point out that even in the face of harsh condemnation, they do consider the reproaches to make sure that they are not missing some grain of truth in the criticisms.

Susan also disputes the words of naysayers. Recognizing that society, in general, considers that individuals with disabilities have low prospects; Susan is convinced that she can easily surpass societal expectations. Her response is one of incredulity at the personal affront of disparaging remarks, and she dismisses the discounting words. Susan does not internalize the discriminatory comments, even if they are cruel and hurtful. It is as if she lets the words wash over her. As a result, she does not allow herself to be distracted by such remarks. Rather, she puts aside personal affronts concerning her potential for success and just gets on with the work. Acerbic comments seem to galvanize and energize her efforts to succeed.

Aaron points out the special case when insiders— perhaps well-meaning mentors or other special confidants— express negativism about a project. Noting that advice coming from trusted advisors has to be considered carefully, Aaron suggests that, in such circumstances, he encourages the testing or retesting of project hypotheses to provide additional evidence of merits or the discovery of inadequacies in the plan. After a thorough analysis, if he still believes the project is important and necessary, he dismisses the concerns of even well meaning dissenters and just proceeds with his plan.

Tangible Loss

Anxiety about failure may be more overwhelming when tangible losses, such as money or possessions, are at stake. Alternatively, such fear may increase because of the potential loss of prestige, diminishment in status, or societal ridicule. In any of these cases, when the loss is considered substantial, courage is required to proceed.

Aaron addresses another point about loss. He says, "If you have nothing, and you are just trying to build something, there is really no relative risk—if your efforts fail, you are left with nothing [what you had before]." Therefore, individuals who take action on their creative ideas early in their careers may not consider the risk to be substantial because they have not acquired a financial standing or established a significant eminence. As a result, they may believe they have less to lose.

Persistence

The MacArthur Fellows interviewed all believe that persistence is a cornerstone that supports success. They also describe synonyms of persistence—patience, perseverance, and tenacity. The interviewees particularly noted the importance of patience over time, perseverance in dealing with rejection and opposition, and tenacity when facing danger.

Patience Over Time

Wes has been working for decades (since 1976) on his plan to reinvent and rehabilitate agriculture. He is interested in providing a compelling alternative to farmers by developing perennial grain species for commercial use. However, he knows that the goals he pursues will not be fulfilled in his lifetime and that he needs to recruit others who believe in the mission of The Land Institute to carry on the work when he is gone.

The pace of progress towards goals, however, does not discourage Wes. He notes, "If the goals you have set for yourself can be accomplished in your lifetime, you are not thinking big enough." Wes sets a high bar in both patience and persistence.

Wilma's patience and persistence is legendary. In her line of work, it can take years to bring a case to court, adjudicate it, and have a final decision. Furthermore, the cleanup of toxic sites is often delayed and, even when finally started, may take many years to complete. Wilma looks at the completion of a case in terms of decades, but she is willing to pursue the polluters until the cleanup is complete.

Perseverance in Dealing With Rejection and Opposition

When it comes to the subject of persistence, Aaron does not mince his words. He explains the importance of persistence in promoting creativity and overall success in life. He says, "If you do not have persistence, you won't be able to surpass or overcome whatever challenges present themselves." More emphatically, he states, "Persistence is the absolute key to success."

Some years ago, Aaron wrote a book about his life experiences. He received a letter from a potential publisher who said that his submission was "one of the worst drafts that he [the publisher] had ever seen." Although that publisher discounted his work in such a disparaging and belittling way, Aaron did not give up his dream to publish. Aaron's persistence paid off when he published the book entitled *Uncommon Rhythm*.[39] To memorialize the initial publisher's harsh and cruel words of rejection, Aaron framed the severely critical letter and hung it on his office wall. In the same area, he also displays a copy of his completed book—edited and published by another company.

Tenacity When Facing Danger

Wilma demonstrates persistence in another way. She has made some enemies—enemies who don't like how she brings corporate polluters to the attention of the public. As a result of her work, she is often harassed, and her office has been burglarized on a number of occasions. A drive-by shooter even interrupted her work by firing at her through her office window. On another occasion, when Wilma was to speak at a meeting, the potential for violence was so great that her client hired a bodyguard to escort her to and from the contentious meeting. However, Wilma is stoic in her belief that the work is paramount, and she will not be deterred by obstacles.

---

[39] A. Dworkin, *Uncommon Rhythm* (Detroit, MI: Aquarius Press, 2011).

Action

The research literature on creativity has not traditionally identified the propensity to take action as a creative characteristic. The MacArthur Fellows, however, recognize that action is a critical step in creativity. Each of the interviewees is committed to turning an idea into an actual outcome.

Action is an essential part of creativity because originality requires both ideas and action. Creative thoughts, alone, cannot have a positive impact on the human experience. Since action is the key to successful creativity, inaction—that which may be termed *dreaming*—represents only an idealized conception that will not result in success.

History has documented the success of many creative individuals, but those who have failed to transform their creative ideas into action have generally not been remembered or celebrated. Their creative thinking has been lost because they failed to take the final step—action.

Aaron describes the need for action in this way. He says, "MacArthur [the MacArthur Foundation] isn't awarding people because they sat around and had great ideas; it's because they put those ideas into action." He continues by saying, "We look at this in our young people and I talk to them all the time—I . . . [say] it's absolutely great to have talent, but it's meaningless unless you realize it." Aaron is adamant; unless an individual takes action to implement a creative idea, there can be no measurable success. His final point is that dreaming without action represents "folly and waste."

Saul adds that his determination to take action is fueled by the understanding that there is much to be accomplished in life and that life is short. He recognizes that time spent without action is wasted.

Wes' words about action emphasize another point. He stresses that action is the only way that change can be accomplished. He does not want to be limited to pumping his fist and saying "ain't it awful." Rather, he is interested in taking action so that he can participate in change.

Susan reinforces the concept that good ideas coupled with action can yield great successes, and she is unwilling to stall action without good reason. For instance, she doesn't consider inexperience an excuse for inaction. She is also not concerned that others might be able to do a better job. Rather than being limited by the prospect that others might be more skilled, Susan says, "If someone has a better idea and can do it better, then so be it. Let them bring it on." Susan's overall message is that perfection, especially on the first attempt, is not required and should not be the goal.

Susan's penchant for taking action has led her to expand her mission at MIUSA. The organization sponsors an annual leadership conference that brings women with disabilities from around the world together to strengthen their leadership capacity, create new visions, and build international networks of support. This gathering of likeminded women embraces the Loud, Proud and Passionate® theme of the conference and helps women move forward to take up personal and professional roles as community, national, and world leaders. Susan wants these women to become part of a pipeline of leaders with disabilities who are crucial participants in the fight to alleviate poverty, achieve gender equality, and claim justice for all individuals with disabilities.

Wilma also comments on the need for action. She, however, focuses on both the need to initiate and the need to continue action. Wilma's view of taking action is reminiscent of the adage by Brian Tracy who discusses the *buffet line of life* where it is necessary to first *get in line* and, then, to be persistent and *stay in line*. He recognizes that individuals are responsible for their own success in life.

Aaron makes another point about the failure to take action. He says, "I think, too often, people don't look at the risk of inaction." In such circumstances, Aaron speculates that a failure to take action might lead to regrets. At one point, he poses a series of rhetorical questions about what he might say to himself as he reflects on his accomplishments in life: "Will I have done what I wanted to do? Will I feel like I didn't squander my time or spend it in a way other than what I would have wanted to do?" Aaron is pointing out that since action is an essential part of creativity, courage may also be necessary to bolster action. Moreover, the courage to act requires faith—faith in one's own abilities.

The general theme expressed by the MacArthur Fellows interviewed is that projects that are only *thought experiments*—not connected with action—are not very interesting. These creative individuals are unwilling to waste their talents on ideas or projects that cannot be converted—for whatever reason—into action. Moreover, they have the courage to take action apropos their creative ideas because they are aware that failure may mean that life goals won't be achieved.

CHAPTER SIX

STRATEGIES AND PROCESSES
THAT SUPPORT CREATIVITY

Creativity doesn't involve sitting back waiting for a flash of insight and doesn't involve wishing for inspiration. Instead, creativity involves the development of distinct strategies and processes that support an individual's innate ability to produce novel outcomes. In effect, the strategies and processes strengthen creativity.

The approaches used to increase creativity may vary among individuals. However, those who regularly create novel outcomes can often explain the routines they employ as they search for creative solutions. Following are some of the strategies and processes that the MacArthur Fellows describe as helpful in their search for creativity.

Big Picture Thinking

One strategy that the MacArthur Fellows use to better understand a problem is *big picture thinking*. This strategy refers to the conscious way that an individual metaphorically steps back from a situation to see the bigger issues of a problem implicit in the circumstances. To do this, the MacArthur Fellows employ an expansive thinking style. They consider issues in the broadest terms and look for ways to define the problem in a comprehensive and inclusive manner that considers the important parameters, internal characteristics, and details of the situation.

Those who approach the world by looking at the big picture tend to ask more questions. By always asking questions, more information can be absorbed, but more problems may also be identified. Creativity has a habit of emerging when new problems are found or reconfigured to give a better understanding of essential aspects of the situation.

To formulate a creative solution, a problem must be conceptualized correctly. Therefore, assumptions about the problem must be examined and verified. If assumptions about the nature of the problem are not carefully considered, a priori suppositions may overshadow and obscure a full understanding of the situation. If imperfect understanding is not corrected, possible creative options may be overlooked.

An example of big picture thinking is one that revolutionized the global shipping industry. Malcolm McLean owned a large trucking fleet in North Carolina and was well versed in the costs of shipping by truck. In 1956, McLean sold his trucking company and bought an ocean shipping company that would become known as Sea-Land Shipping. He recognized that moving freight on and off ships was a large expense. The numerous sizes and weights of boxes, bags, barrels, and crates that made up his cargo increased those shipping costs because each type of cargo needed to be handled differently. Additionally, the loading and unloading process subjected the cargo to possible damage or theft.

Taking a step back to look at the problem, and factoring in that much of the freight would later be transported by truck or train, McLean conceived of a way to containerize freight in standard size units. The standardized containers could be relatively easily moved to and from his ships and then could be conveyed with minimum interruption using alternate modes of transport.

Initially, McLean's idea involved transporting containerized freight already loaded on truck trailers. This allowed the trailers to be wheeled onto ships with their cargo. However, McLean soon realized that a simpler configuration for containers would be superior. He devised standardized containers that could be quickly lifted by crane from a vehicle directly onto a ship. Later, this process could be reversed as the containerized product moved across the globe to its ultimate destination.

McLean's thoughtful look at the issues surrounding the loading and unloading of freight onto various conveyances revolutionized the shipping industry and global trade. In addition to creating the standardized container, he modified his ships and terminals so that he could maximize the number of containers processed, thereby further reducing loading and unloading times and costs.

Domain History and Its Relationship to Creativity

In discussing big picture thinking, Saul endorses the idea that studying the history of a problem can also help promote a better understanding of the situation. He points out that people who are preeminent and notably creative in their fields are also extremely knowledgeable about the history of their specific area(s) of expertise. Specifically, such experts have studied the pioneering scientists who did initial domain research. Understanding extends to not only the *why* and *what* of a field, but also the *when* and *who*. The assumptions and theories of earlier work provide context and can result in the recognition of failures in past understanding. Armed with such information, Saul believes he is better able to discern creative solutions to complex problems.

Furthermore, studying history can identify instances where nonexistent or insufficient technology hampered early scientists who sought to advance theories. For instance, without the power of computers, earlier researchers were often faced with mountains of data to compute manually and no practical way to solve equations. However, improvements in computational power now allow complex mathematical equations to be solved accurately and more quickly—helping current scientists verify and dispute past hypotheses.

Wes also points out how he used his knowledge of agricultural history to better understand how customary farming techniques, established in ancient times and which are part of numerous religious traditions, have promoted significant soil erosion and negatively affected the environment. Moreover, in more recent times, large agricultural corporations, still not comprehending the inherent problem of traditional farming techniques, have increased the devastation by enlarging the scale of agriculture. Through his understanding of the history of agriculture and his extensive training in biology, botany, and genetics, Wes recognizes that continuing current farming practices will increase environmental devastation. This understanding prompted Wes to promote a fundamentally different agriculture. The Land Institute, which Wes directs, recommends growing perennial crops. Such crops reduce the need to annually till and replant fields and, therefore, reduce soil erosion.

More recently, Transatomic Power has explored the history of nuclear energy to discover or rediscover new ways to produce nuclear power. While there is a general understanding that energy produced from nuclear material is cheap relative to many other forms of energy, there is a continuing concern around the safety of the technology. Additionally, there is a concern that stored nuclear waste will present increasing problems over the next decades, centuries, and millennia during which time the waste will remain hazardous.

Fortunately, Transatomic Power, a company that proposes to solve the two big concerns of nuclear energy production—safe nuclear reactor operation and safe storage of spent nuclear fuel—is developing a process of using residual or spent nuclear fuel in a safer molten salt reactor that will produce reliable and dependable nuclear energy. The technology used in molten salt reactors has been around a long time, but it was passed over when light water nuclear reactors became the more conventional approach to producing nuclear energy. However, now Transatomic Power has reevaluated the value of the molten salt reactors. Improved materials and modern technology that make the reactor more compact, affordable, and power dense will allow the company to assuage safety concerns surrounding the use of nuclear materials and also reduce building and startup costs. Moreover, Transatomic Power has developed a way to use spent nuclear material that has been discarded (and expensively stored) to fuel their reactors. These improvements could breathe new life into the nuclear power industry.

Dr. Leslie Dewan and Mark Massie, both graduates of MIT's Nuclear Engineering Department, lead the efforts of Transatomic Power. By taking the time to step back and consider the big picture view of nuclear power production and by looking at the history that created the problems in the industry, they have determined how modern materials and techniques can solve the difficulties. Their creativity may be the key to the rejuvenation of an industry that will be able to provide safe, low-cost energy for the world.

Reframing a Problem

Another strategy that may be helpful in promoting creativity is reframing. The process of reframing a problem is multifaceted. However, in the context of better understanding creativity, reframing is about changing perspective. Reframing challenges an individual to see things differently. The perspective change can be either mental or physical, but the goal, in either case, is to clarify and refresh the prevailing viewpoint.

When a reframing strategy is used, those involved in the process may come to an agreement on more precise definitions and thereby gain a better understanding of ambiguous terminology, which can clarify either goals or situation parameters. Additionally, if incomplete or faulty problem framing is corrected or tangentially related concepts are identified in the reframing exercise, new insights may suggest new solutions.

A World War II situation illustrates how reframing can impact understanding. In 1942, the Allied command was making plans to retake Europe through France. There was, however, a formidable problem. The Germans had occupied and fortified all of the French deep-water ports, making invasion through those ports impossible. The situation was also complicated because Allied invading forces could disembark at most coastal points, but the deep-keeled boats that were necessary to transport the heavy and bulky cargo of armaments and supplies needed to support the invasion would require a deep-water port and dockside cranes to offload the supply ships' cargo.

The Allied answer to this conundrum was the secret creation of the Mulberry Artificial Harbor. Vice Admiral John Hughes-Hallett envisioned a portable harbor complete with cranes and other anchorage requirements. His unique concept of a portable harbor represents an example of creative thinking where a problem was recast to suggest a novel solution. If a deep-water port was necessary and none were to be had on the French coast, a harbor needed to be built in England and transported across the English Channel to serve the invading forces. The decision was made to secretly build the Mulberry Artificial Harbor and transport it across the English Channel. Final installation was completed just weeks after Allied forces invaded France on June 6, 1944.

The Mulberry Artificial Harbor was an essential link that supported the invasion. It provided facilities needed to offload critical armaments—including tanks, armored vehicles, and ammunition—as well as food and medical necessities that had to be at hand to support the advancing forces. Port Winston, the Mulberry Artificial Harbor that was installed at Arromanches, France, saw heavy use. In the 10 months after D-Day, it was used to land over 2.5 million men, 500,000 vehicles, and 4 million tons of supplies for the Allied army in France.

This story illustrates how reframing can change perspective. Initially, the problem seemed to concern the availability of a coastal harbor. However, when the idea of what constitutes a harbor was investigated and reframed, an alternate solution was imagined. In other words, a better understanding of the reality of the problem broadened the scope and led to thinking differently about the issue. The lesson is that those who seek creative outputs need to expand their thinking to carefully examine the essential tenets of a problem, verifying the accuracy and appropriateness of stated and unstated goals.

In many instances, reframing can be triggered by *why* questions. If there is no answer to a why question or if answers seem insufficient or inconsequential, consider looking for a reframing opportunity that makes the situation easier to understand. Investigating why questions should test both the norms and other a priori assumptions that make up the dominant viewpoint. The process may be iterative in the sense that multiple norms and assumptions may need to be examined.

A change of perspective can also be accomplished by taking into account the views of others. Sometimes, the way that other people view a problem can expand the frame, help detect alternate issues and considerations, and lead to a refinement of assumptions and goals.

In her book, *Uncommon Genius,* Denise Shekerjian provides a fine reframing example.[40] The consulting group of Arthur D. Little was working with a client who wanted to develop a new kind of can opener. Broadening the concept of *opening* led to a reframing opportunity. The pea pod inspired the group to consider non-mechanical options, which included plastic strips to open juice cans and the biscuit batter tube that pops open when struck on a counter edge. Such reframing can be beneficial in expanding alternatives and may provide the next logical step that can lead to a creative solution.

---

[40] D. Shekerjian, *Uncommon Genius* (New York, NY: Penguin, 1990).

Reframing may also occur as a result of a better understanding of underlying problem configurations or concerns. When Saul is working on a problem, he finds it helpful to look at the scientific principles associated with the problem and express them in more generalized and overarching statements that explain the situation in terms of a physical system. If flawed reasoning is detected in the explanation of the physical system, there probably is a need to reevaluate how the system is conceived. When additional analysis is complete, a more nuanced and corrected lens for understanding might be hypothesized.

Saul utilized this process of reframing to improve the effectiveness of natural gas storage for use in automobiles. As he considered how to store the fuel, he noticed that designs incorporated a large natural gas reservoir that had the shape of a tank used for scuba diving. Saul believed that tanks for storing natural gas did not need to be large in diameter and that the adoption of the tank shape represented a flawed assumption.

Having discerned the faulty scientific assumption, Saul reconsidered the problem. He replaced the large and unwieldy tank design with one that stored the same amount of natural gas in a small diameter chamber, albeit long, that could be folded to fit into an automobile infrastructure. The tank, in effect, became part of the automobile chassis. When Saul clarified the problem, the solution was more readily discerned.

In current times, there is another product—bicycles— that might benefit from a redesign based on reframing. Bicycles are still designed and built based on old perspectives. Before the days of aluminum bicycle frames, and long before the use of carbon fiber, bicycles all had horizontal crossbars that connected the seat and handlebar assemblies because crossbars provided essential strength to the overall frame. When women began riding, this horizontal bar was slanted down to allow mounting and dismounting while wearing dresses. The slanted bar compromised the strength of the bicycle frame, but, apparently, modifying the crossbar was considered acceptable, as it wasn't very ladylike for women to ride their bikes as roughly as men.

Based on stronger construction materials, today's bicycles no longer need a horizontal crossbar. Yet, current models of men's bicycles still incorporate this stabilizing design element, although there is no technical reason for doing so. Moreover, such bars may be hazardous to the riders if a foot should slip off a pedal. In this situation, while a newer design is more advantageous, old framing and habits still endure.

The Relatedness of the Seemingly Unrelated

Examining the relationship of situational elements has also helped the MacArthur Fellows interviewed find creative solutions. They describe the process as looking for the "relatedness of the seemingly unrelated." Wes talks about his experience, saying that he likes to turn traditional "notions on their heads" with the aim of finding creative combinations that can enhance creativity.

In the 1970s, before Wes created The Land Institute, he had been reading a General Accounting Office study on soil erosion and that report worried him because, despite conservation measures, soil erosion continued and was as ecologically detrimental as the 1930s Dust Bowl that created barren fields. After reading the troubling report, Wes took his university students on a field trip to the Konza Prairie—a tall grass prairie preserve jointly owned by the Nature Conservancy and Kansas State University. Wes noted that, unlike the grain cropland that experienced significant soil erosion, the prairie was healthy and naturally fertile. When he examined the two situations in his mind, he realized that the major difference was that farmers planting annual grain crops seasonally tilled the soil and that the natural prairie that supported perennials was never tilled. Bringing together the concepts of farmers' fields and natural prairie growth with the concern about soil erosion caused by the tilling of fields gave Wes a moment of clarity that prompted him to create The Land Institute.

In addition to recognizing that the natural prairie was healthy and the cultivated land was shedding tons of soil due to tilling processes, Wes recognized the natural prairie as inherently healthier because its polycultural vegetation was more sustainable. Again, the comparison of the natural prairie to cultivated fields led Wes to understand that crop variation found on the prairie reduced issues of fungal, insect, and blight infestation. Recognizing the issue as important, Wes developed more clarity about why large agricultural corporations that plant monocultures must use more chemicals to combat various crop infestations.

Jim also explained how he had brought together unrelated ideas when he developed a machine that could decipher and read text for individuals who have difficulties making use of printed books. As he considered the problem, Jim recalled that in one of his most exciting engineering classes at Caltech he learned how to design technology that would allow a computer to distinguish various sorts of military targets (e.g., different types of military tanks). The weapons systems in his class project could direct munitions to strike specific targets and had the underlying ability to recognize distinct target configurations. Considering his new conundrum, Jim recognized the parallels in the unrelated projects. If computers could distinguish between military targets, couldn't they also distinguish the shapes of letters?

Using the same base technology, Jim developed a reading machine—the optical character reader. The optical character recognition (OCR) technology was similar to the tank-targeting technology except that instead of distinguishing between various types of military tanks, the computer was tasked with identifying specific letters of the alphabet. Despite the obvious differences (in size, shape, and purpose) between military tanks and letters, Jim was able to understand that the same computer technology could solve both problems. By seeing the relationship between the two problems, he was able to envision new uses for the tank-targeting technology.

The development of the automobile airbag provides two examples of how unrelated concepts were combined into new configurations that led to novel products. The first instance involved John Hetrick, who considered the importance of protecting automobile passengers in the event of a front-end collision. He remembered an incident during his WWII U.S. military service when he was repairing a torpedo. During the repair process, a sudden release of compressed air inflated the torpedo's canvas cover, shooting the torpedo and its bag to the ceiling. From this experience, Hetrick was able to conceive of inflation through compressed air as a component of his *safety cushion* for cars—the forerunner of today's airbags.

A second inventor, Allen Breed, was also able to improve automobile airbags by combining unrelated ideas. Breed, who had significant experience in fuses and sensor technology gained while working for the U.S. military, was able to recognize that while the concepts of *explosion* and *trigger* were common in the military munitions business, they could also be applied to the controlled detonation needed for safety cushions. He was able to imagine a new safety device that was conceptually simple; accelerometers triggered the ignition of a gas propellant to rapidly inflate a nylon bag. This new use of an older military technology converted a life-taking capability into a lifesaving one.

Combining unrelated ideas was also instrumental in the development of a common kitchen convenience—food storage bags. Ziploc technology was originally used to seal pencils into cases that were attached to 3-ring binders. Borge Madsen was granted a patent for his slide fastener in 1951. However, the locking zipper technology gained traction and became a multibillion-dollar product when it was used to close plastic food storage bags. George F. Kirkpatrick improved the closure mechanisms by using different colors for the zipper components. In his version of the product, the zipper changed color when the bag was successfully closed.

The process of exploring the relatedness of the seemingly unrelated has helped many individuals create novel outcomes. *Bringing together disparate ideas* is another name for this experience. Whatever term is used to describe the strategy, it represents the combining of alternate perspectives that can provoke novel connections between ideas that come from different fields. Such connections are characterized by a result that can be described as having an *unexpected twist*.

Tolerance for Ambiguity

Feelings of ambiguity may develop in situations where questions don't have obvious answers.[41] Ambiguity can generate a vague sense of personal uneasiness that can feel oppressive. Nevertheless, if seeking to be creative, it is necessary to learn to accept the uneasy feeling of ambiguity until a full and uncensored range of potential problem solutions can surface in the mind and be evaluated. Rather than accepting an adequate

[41] T. Kristensen, "The Physical Context of Creativity," *Creativity and Innovation Management* 13, no. 2 (2004): 89-96.

solution, having the ability to tolerate ambiguity can allow the best alternative to emerge from disordered ideas and can result in the selection of an optimal answer. However, when quick decisions are taken to reduce or remove the uneasiness of ambiguity, the result may be suboptimal.

The MacArthur Fellows interviewed describe how they consciously make an effort to tolerate a state of uncertainty during their creative processes. As they search for a problem solution, the MacArthur Fellows deliberately tolerate ambiguity by maintaining an *openness* in the face of confusing, contradictory, or vague information. According to the interviewees, such openness can support creativity and discourage adopting solutions that reflect only incremental improvement. This is important because decisions that offer only incremental improvement are only adequate and do not promote truly creative outcomes. In effect, passable, satisfactory, or tolerable solutions represent the antithesis of creativity. However, if an individual is willing to trust the process and tolerate ambiguity, the disorder that causes personal discomfort will gradually transform to order as the best ideas are understood and implemented.

Wes claims that ambiguity is important in his creative process. He comments, "If we are going to count ourselves as grownups, we've got to be able to tolerate ambiguity."

Susan loves the feeling because it means that she can consider multiple answers without judgment of right or wrong. This frees her to consider a wider range of possibilities.

Ambiguity, she admits, can feel like chaos, but she is certain that order will be reestablished, taking her a step closer to a creative solution. Susan also notes that tolerating ambiguity is the ability to initiate a plan without having decided all of the details. She points out that proceeding without all particulars defined is not for the faint of heart, but that embarking on such a journey is not frightening if you have confidence that you will figure out the steps as you go.

The key to tolerating ambiguity is to accept that answers to a problem may be elusive in the present, but that further study and analysis will likely bring forward creative solutions. In effect, this developmental phase is part of the creative process—a phase that needs to be embraced.

Allowing for Incubation

Having a tolerance for ambiguity may delay coming to a decision. However, this also allows additional time for germane thoughts and ideas to emerge. Kristensen defines this phenomenon as *incubation*.[42] A state of ambiguity allows an idea to incubate in a person's brain so that a problem solution may emerge over time.

Saul indicates that he depends on incubation as he searches for creative answers. Recognizing that he can't force creative solutions to emerge, he works on multiple projects at one time. In this way, he can give his mind time to incubate

---

[42] T. Kristensen, "The Physical Context of Creativity," *Creativity and Innovation Management* 13, no. 2 (2004): 89-96.

ideas on one project as he moves forward on another. Just giving his mind a rest also helps. To do so, Saul turns to hobbies and play to relax his mind. By engaging his brain in a new endeavor, he is able to stop the continuous internal chatter. However, his brain is working in the background on problems, and, over time, alternative ideas and solutions will likely rise to consciousness.

Mihaly Csikszentmihalyi describes how incubation can improve creative output.[43] Freeman Dyson, a student of well-known physicist Richard Feynman, decided that to advance the study of physics, he must integrate the work of his mentor with the work of another eminent physicist, Julian Schwinger. Each scientist was working on the unification of quantum and electrodynamics principles, but each approached the work differently and each had a different way of expressing the scientific outcomes of the work. Dyson set out to bring the efforts of the two scientists together so that the laws of electrodynamics might be understood in terms of the principles of quantum mechanics.

Colleagues of Feynman considered his work important, but Feynman's work was not always organized enough to garner support from other scientists who might have replicated his efforts. Schwinger's work was at the other end of the spectrum. He worked very methodically to resolve the issues of his research, but he was always hesitant to claim a solution. As a

---

[43] M. Csikszentmihalyi, *Creativity* (New York, NY: Harper Collins, 1996).

result, little progress was being made on the problems of quanta and their relationship to electrical phenomena.

After 6 months of calculating and reviewing the works of Feynman and Schwinger, Dyson went on vacation. As he returned home, Dyson experienced an epiphany concerning the work of the two physicists. He was able to reconcile the work of Feynman and Schwinger, hypothesizing how the work of each scientist fit together into a useful theory. His vacation represented a period of incubation that allowed time for his mind to sort out and arrange aspects of each scientist's work. Feynman and Schwinger, along with Sin-Itiro Tomonaga, shared the Nobel Prize in Physics in 1965; however, many experts in the domain considered Dyson's efforts to be equally important to the understanding of the work.

A better understanding of incubation can also clarify why some individuals believe that the emergence of creativity is precipitated by an *aha* moment. While an idea may come to consciousness in one specific moment, the process of getting to a creative resolution has probably occurred over a longer time. It is simply that the recognition of the solution happens in a moment. Csikszentmihalyi suggests that insight occurs when "a subconscious connection between ideas fits so well that it is forced to pop out into awareness, like a cork held underwater breaking out into the air after it is released."[44]

---

[44] M. Csikszentmihalyi, *Creativity* (New York, NY: Harper Collins, 1996), 104.

Each of the strategies and processes discussed in this chapter help the MacArthur Fellows enhance their creativity. Big picture thinking, understanding domain history, problem reframing, investigating the relatedness of the seemingly unrelated, having a tolerance for ambiguity, and allowing time for incubation are all proven approaches that support creative outcomes. Sometimes the interviewees even use multiple strategies in one project. However, the list is not presented as the only approach to creativity. Additional strategies and processes may also have merit. Therefore, the list should serve as a beginning point in the development of personal strategies and processes that support a search for creative solutions.

CHAPTER SEVEN

THE ESSENTIALS OF CREATIVITY

This book is about understanding how creativity is activated, developed, and sustained in individuals. Fortunately, the individual MacArthur Fellows interviewed have carefully considered their own personal processes of creativity. As a result, they are self-aware and able to describe in detail the ways that they approach their own work in the search for creative outcomes. The following conclusions summarize themes developed in the dissertation research and detailed in this book.

Work Is a Passion

All of the MacArthur Fellows interviewed have a passion for their work. Recognizing that passion for a subject promotes and accelerates their creative success, they only pursue work about which they are enthusiastic. They are locked into their work—focused, driven, and joyful.

The interviewees have chosen to do what they love, and, according to them, everyone else should choose a joyful vocation too. Settling for a career that only provides a paycheck and little satisfaction is anathema for the MacArthur Fellows because settling will not only inhibit creativity, but also will forestall a full and enriching life. Consider the dentist who has established a successful practice but doesn't really like the work or the attorney who was initially enamored with studying law but is fatigued and bored in the role of lawyer. These are common occurrences in society. It is not likely that those who feel trapped within a profession or field will find creativity in their future. Additionally, they are unlikely to find much satisfaction. If experiencing a professional malaise, the MacArthur Fellows suggest facing this reality and finding a new path. Fortunately, those unhappy with their established roles can still adapt, seeking a new role in another domain that feels more aligned and gives more personal satisfaction.

The MacArthur Fellows interviewed are also vibrant and exuberant individuals who take their work seriously—working methodically and systematically to be creative. It seems as if the MacArthur Fellows are doing exactly what they want to do, and they do not experience their jobs as work in a traditional sense. Rather, their work enriches them, encouraging more effort and joy in the process. Part of this joy comes from choosing a domain that not only excites but for which they have an enduring love.

Perspiration Is Essential

The love for their work creates a dogged work ethic in the MacArthur Fellows. Those interviewed don't describe a flash of creative insight that heralds advancement in their work; rather, they suggest that the diligent pursuit of possibility is the key. Persistence is essential. Consistent with Thomas Edison's adage—"Genius is 1% inspiration and 99% perspiration"[45]—the analysis of interviews with the MacArthur Fellows suggests that perspiration, used as a synonym for persistence, is the key to creativity. Of all the insights that the fellows shared, this concept that persistence provides the platform for creative outcomes is their most strongly advocated theme.

Confident but Not Egotistical

All of the MacArthur Fellows interviewed are confident individuals—confident in their ability to produce creative outcomes. However, not one is egotistical. Not one proposes having the only possible or even the most creative response to a need. Not one suggests that he or she is the most intelligent person in the room.

It might even be said that these creative individuals are humble. They deflect personal accolades about their success. Some even express surprise that the MacArthur Foundation would consider their work creative. Wilma, for example, said that the award announcement was personally gratifying and, yet, completely unanticipated.

The interviewees repeatedly give credit to others in their fields, especially those who have come before them. They are also likely to praise individuals within their organizations. Wes speaks highly of his colleagues and is quick to give them credit for ideas, which support the development of his work. Susan

---

[45] C. Edison, "The Electric Thomas Edison," in *Reader's Digest: Great Lives, Great Deeds* (Pleasantville, NY: Reader's Digest, 1964), 204.

claims that her organization's success could not have been accomplished without the work of her team. Saul repeatedly acknowledges colleagues and mentors and even extends his gratitude to company interns for work well done. When I sent drafts of my dissertation data analysis to the interviewees, the most common edits were to expand their thoughts on a subject and to extend credit to others with whom they have collaborated.

Respect for Diverse Opinions

The MacArthur Fellows interviewed are not only modest about their own contributions and respectful of the efforts of others, but they also value alternate approaches to work. For instance, there is no demonizing of contemporaries based on personal foibles, no dismissal of others because they speak about issues differently or employ different methods to gain results, and no petty negativity. All study participants show respect for the work of others and acknowledge diverse opinions.

With no time lost discounting eccentricities or quarrelling with others, the fellows have more time to concentrate on important projects. This respect for diverse opinions is important. Alternate perspectives come from individuals who have different lived experiences, and the MacArthur Fellows understand that diversity can enhance creative efforts in their fields. Ultimately, learning comes from many sources.

Full-Blast Living

The MacArthur Fellows interviewed give the impression that they live their values, are dedicated to their chosen work, and are optimistic about the future. As they talk about creativity, they describe a practice directed by cognitive effort and specific processes and strengthened by an understanding that there is a great need for problem solutions. In effect, the MacArthur Fellows interviewed are not only committed to finding creative outcomes, but they are also interested in living creative lives.

The desire for creative expression is in the excitement of a revelation, the thrill of solving a problem, and the recognition that a creation can be an elegant response to a problem. In addition, creativity is about improving society and doing what's right. Money and fame do not seem to be motivators.

The fellows have also developed resilience. Resilience, for them, represents a combination of characteristics that embody the spirit of an individual. Included are the abilities to recover from discouragement and setbacks, cope with loss, and keep striving in the face of adversity. Additionally, resilience is connected with each MacArthur Fellow's capacity for adapting to change. Resilience also includes the idea that improvisation may be necessary to navigate around and through problems. Individuals who are resilient are also inclined to take risks and have dispositions that are flexible and pliable, minds that are open to possibility, and an enduring personal commitment to goals that may be observed as dogged perseverance.

All of the fellows interviewed are barely restrained bundles of energy. Each is a whirlwind that seeks new avenues of creative action. Yet, the fellows are very different from each other in many ways. Saul is a veteran iconoclast and doesn't mince his words on any subject. Sometimes, his expressions of emotion challenged my ability to paraphrase his sentiments, as his language was often salty—to put it mildly. Victoria speaks eloquently, using beautiful metaphors to make her point. It makes me smile to think of Saul and Victoria conversing.

Fortunately, the fellows were easy to contact. I did a quick search on the Internet and easily found personal email addresses. Also, I had quick and positive responses to my interview requests. I sent one potential study participant an email at 7:00 a.m. in the hopes that he would see it as soon as he got to his office. Apparently, 7:00 in the morning isn't early; he answered my email in seconds, accepting my request for an interview to be conducted within a week.

This was not an exception; the MacArthur Fellows interviewed were quick to respond and were happy to engage in the research. They quickly understood the goals of the study and joined me as if they were co-investigators in the search for clues to the nature of creativity. They were extremely generous with their time and really seemed to want to share their personal approach to creativity knowing that their efforts would support my research. Their collegial engagement style emphasized their unremitting search for knowledge and their empathy for a researcher.

Additionally, the interviewees' willingness to support my research represents their respect and appreciation for the work of the MacArthur Foundation. Without exception, the interviewees expressed their admiration for the work of the foundation and stated how meaningful the award is to them.

No One Formula for Creativity

There is no defined and perfected strategy or process that can be implemented to ensure the development of creative outcomes. Detailed approaches that specify steps or rote checklists that define creative stages are, by their nature, decidedly uncreative. However, broad strategies and processes have been helpful to the MacArthur Fellows—allowing them a way to *connect the dots* in a search for creative solutions.

While these specific strategies and processes work for the MacArthur Fellows, they do not represent the only approach to creativity: instead, they are examples of discrete methods that have successfully stimulated creativity in others. In effect, the MacArthur Fellows' strategies and processes may be an appropriate starting place to seek creative outcomes. However, individuals should not be constrained by the approaches detailed in this book. Rather, an individual's goal should be to discover the most effective ways to activate, develop, and sustain personal creativity—recognizing that this is a highly subjective practice.

The personal characteristics and habits that the MacArthur Fellows have cultivated also help them produce creative outcomes. Once again there is no definitive checklist of characteristics or habits that accurately promotes creative success. However, the reader can gain insight into creativity by evaluating the attributes that the MacArthur Fellows value.

CHAPTER EIGHT

FINAL INSIGHTS

As this book comes to a close, I present one final thought about the MacArthur Fellows and their creativity. Robert Frost, a former U.S. poet laureate, wrote about the need to understand the connections in life. In his poem, *Two Tramps in Mudtime*, Frost wrote:

> *But yield who will to their separation,*
> *My object in living is to unite*
> *My avocation with my vocation*
> *As my two eyes make one in sight.*
> *Only where love and need are one,*
> *And the work is play for mortal stakes,*
> *Is the deed ever really done*
> *For heaven and the future's sakes.*

This final stanza of Frost's poem reminds readers of the relationship between *avocation* and *vocation* and of the importance of bringing together *love* and *need* and *work* and *play* in their lives. Interestingly, the MacArthur Fellows live by Frost's words. Having carved out important goals to serve the world, they also take advantage of their love for the work so that their labor feels like play.

The MacArthur Fellows interviewed also understand that the world needs their creativity. They know that the inhabitants of planet Earth face increasingly complex problems. The global nature of environmental issues, population growth, disease, and geopolitics make it increasingly difficult to implement effective solutions. However, the absolute existence of humankind depends on creative solutions being developed and implemented. In order to continue to thrive on Earth, humankind must come to the realization that we *play* for exceedingly important, if not, *mortal stakes.* Those who look for creative solutions need to understand that their work represents deeds done *for heaven and the future's sake.*

A powerful conclusion is that individuals have a responsibility to participate in societal conversations about world problems. Additionally, they have an obligation to seek effective ways to solve problems. This can only occur if individuals are willing to stimulate and engage their personal creativity, discover realistic answers, and leverage their abilities to implement solutions.

In accepting the need to creatively solve problems, recognize that creative individuals are all around. Align with others who aspire to promote their creativity, recognizing that creative energy is contagious.

Finally, as you compose your life, be unwavering in your commitment to seeking creative solutions. This is the foundation for success and fulfillment in your personal and professional life. Strive, risk, discover, pursue, and open your mind to creativity and what's possible.

ACKNOWLEDGEMENTS

Given that this book is based on dissertation research, I would first like to acknowledge the support of my professors at the University of San Diego. In particular, the expertise and experience of my dissertation committee was invaluable in the initial conception and execution of the research. Dr. Robert Donmoyer, Dr. Fred Galloway, and Dr. Lea Hubbard all challenged me throughout the research process. They urged me to look deeper into the results and critically think about their meaning and importance.

I also wish to thank the MacArthur Foundation. As a result of the foundation's years of work identifying and selecting creative award winners, I was able to choose research participants who have been judged to have the creative qualities I was seeking to study. Moreover, the work of the foundation has allowed me to meet inspiring individuals who have had a profound effect on my view of the world.

Ultimately, the research was only feasible with the help of the creative MacArthur Fellows I interviewed. I thank them for their graciousness in accepting my invitation to be interviewed and for their enthusiasm throughout the project. It was their stories I told, and it was only through their revelations that I was able to begin to understand their creative processes. The experience of interacting with the MacArthur Fellows was also an opportunity for me to learn from role models of human achievement. I was inspired by their enthusiasm for life, inquisitive natures, determination to pursue expansive goals, and their passion for and dedication to their work.

Once I conceptualized this book and began synthesizing the information from the dissertation, I had the support of many others. My husband, Randy, provided encouragement and advice throughout the writing. He was a reliable sounding board and this work could not have been accomplished without his sage insights and on-going encouragement. Chris and Alison, my children, played their own part in supporting me in this process of discovery. I was touched that they frequently asked about my progress and encouraged my efforts.

I was also fortunate to have friends and colleagues who enthusiastically commented on first drafts of the book. Marianne Jumago made thoughtful comments and debated the basic structure of the chapters. Joe Turcotte reinforced the importance of the book's subject—noting that after reading the book he was willing to consider the possibility that it might be possible to activate his own creativity. The comments of Dr. Mary McDonald and Dr. Sondra Thiederman helped me identify my target audience and hone the message for them. Joe Franklin and Dottie Harman gave me feedback on their experience of reading the material. This helped me further refine the message. My editor, Susanne Strauss, helped me polish the writing and her expertise was invaluable in creating the final version of the book.

ABOUT THE AUTHOR

 Leslie is committed to continuous learning, especially the study of creativity and problem solving. Her learning motto is: Live every day as if it is your last, pursue learning as if you will live forever.

Believing that the nonprofit sector is best positioned to solve the world's many complex problems, Leslie is dedicated to the sector and teaches courses in Nonprofit Leadership at the University of San Diego.

Leslie has a B.A. in English Literature (University of Colorado), an MBA (University of San Diego), a Masters in Global Studies (Denver University), and a Ph.D. in Leadership Studies (University of San Diego).

Canine Companions for Independence is a favored nonprofit that provides highly trained assistance dogs—free of charge—to people with disabilities. Leslie is a puppy raiser and also serves on the organization's National Board of Directors.

Beyond teaching, researching, and writing, Leslie pursues health and fitness activities and seeks out unconventional travel adventures.

Book Royalties Donated: All royalties from book sales are donated to Canine Companions for Independence (CCI), a 501(c)(3) nonprofit that provides highly trained service dogs free of charge to individuals with disabilities. Donations to CCI are maximized when books are purchased through lulu.com. Books are also available from Amazon.com, BarnesandNoble.com, and Ingramcontent.com

Contact: Leslie.Hennessy@gmail.com

www.ingramcontent.com/pod-product-compliance
Lightning Source LLC
Chambersburg PA
CBHW022017170526
45157CB00003B/1266